When Peter Payne, hero of *The Diary of a Teenage Health Freak*, was informing the world of his worries about acne and the length of certain parts of his anatomy, little did he realize that before long his younger sister Susie would try to outshine him with a diary of her own.

Now an experienced and fully mobiled 16-year-old, Susie writes about sex, romance, anorexia, glandular fever, depression, death, Aids, dieting, taking exams, animal rights, contraception, divorce, coping with stress, and many things besides. In her diary she includes cuttings, leaflets, letters, emails, text messages, and other bits and pieces about the problems that concern her, along with the latest exclusive reports on her brother Pete's continuing relationships and health problems. Based on carefully researched medical facts, her diary provides bang up-to-date information that is guaranteed to entertain and inform teenagers of all ages.

When her diary first appeared, the atmosphere in the Payne household was somewhat strained for a few days: Pete – ever jealous of his sister's abilities – made rude comments (although he was secretly impressed); there was a frosty reception from her parents; and at least one ex-boyfriend changed his name and went to live abroad. Bovril the cat just smiled enigmatically, silently relishing the thought of what would happen if she wrote a cat's-eye view of what the Payne family really got up to.

But after Susie's diary was first published (initially in a somewhat censored form), the phone soon started to ring and the letters flooded in: Pete began to enjoy basking in reflected glory; her parents started recommending it to their friends; and new boyfriends appeared. Teenagers all over the world said, 'Great! Is there any more?' So Susie has at last, in this third edition, agreed to publish a full and uncensored version. Bovril is still biding her time.

**AIDAN MACFARLANE** ran the Child and Adolescent Health services for the Oxfordshire Health Authority. He is now an international freelance consultant in child and adolescent health.

**ANN McPHERSON** is a general practitioner with extensive experience of young people and their problems, and a lecturer in the Department of Primary Health Care at the University of Oxford.

As well as *The Diary of a Teenage Health Freak* and its sequel *The Diary of the Other Health Freak*, their other books include *Mum I Feel Funny* (which won the Times Education Supplement Information Book Award), *Me and My Mates*, *The Virgin Now Boarding*, and *Fresher Pressure*. Most recently they published a book for parents about the teenage years called *Teenagers: the agony, the ecstasy, the answers*.

The authors also run an extremely successful website for teenagers – www.teenagehealthfreak.org – which receives over 150,000 hits a week and recently won the BUPA communication award.

## Acknowledgements

For this, the third edition of *The Diary of the Other Health Freak*, we would again like to thank our researcher, Cathy Boyd, and the thousands of teenagers who emailed our website, www.teenagehealthfreak.org, with their concerns and views on teenage life today. Special thanks also to Oscar Leonard, and Stella, Athene and Thomas Dilke, who went through the book word by word making sure that the language was 'appropriate' for today's teenagers. Also many, many thanks to all the other teenagers who have, over the years, appreciated the book, and freely given their opinions of what was both good and bad about Susie's diary.

Like the previous editions, this edition was once again much aided and abetted by our own children, Beth, Gus, Magnus, Sam, Tess and Tamara, and their friends – though Magnus and Sam were notable for their reluctance to reveal any part of their teenage existence, while still much enjoying the money the books brought in!

Susie's diary is a combination of a large number of different voices and sources. An advertisement in *Just 17* produced an avalanche of pale pink and yellow envelopes, full of wonderful, funny and sometimes libellous stories. Local Oxfordshire school pupils again provided a rich and fruitful source of information.

# The Diary of the Other Health Freak

**Ann McPherson and Aidan Macfarlane**

Illustrated by John Astrop

**OXFORD**
UNIVERSITY PRESS

# OXFORD
## UNIVERSITY PRESS

Great Clarendon Street, Oxford OX2 6DP

Oxford University Press is a department of the University of Oxford.
It furthers the University's objective of excellence in research, scholarship,
and education by publishing worldwide in

Oxford New York

Auckland Bangkok Buenos Aires
Cape Town Chennai Dar es Salaam Delhi Hong Kong Istanbul
Karachi Kolkata Kuala Lumpur Madrid Melbourne Mexico City Mumbai
Nairobi São Paulo Shanghai Taipei Tokyo Toronto

Oxford is a registered trade mark of Oxford University Press
in the UK and in certain other countries

British Library Cataloguing in Publication Data available

ISBN 0-19-910904-4

3 5 7 9 10 8 6 4 2

Printed in the UK
Cox & Wyman Ltd, Reading, Berkshire

# Contents

# Organizing **Boys**, **Sex** and **Work**

**1st January** Messaged Kate: 'Sorry lost mobile. Now OK. Doing new diary. NRN'. Pete gave me the *ltle bk of txt msgs* for Christmas so am hot. But redid message to Kate saying that 'NRN' meant 'No reply necessary'.

Pete thinks I'm being a copycat, keeping my own diary when his is so famous. But I'm going to write down everything that I can think of, exactly as it happens. If I write something wrong, then it'll be like telling lies to myself. That's why I hope this one'll be secret until I decide – unlike the one of mine that Pete was so busy reading and showing off to the outside world. He should've been locked up for that.


**2nd January** Fourteen days to my birthday. Can't wait till I'm 16 when I'll be able to:

» get married with the consent of Mum or Dad (Pete would be delighted to get rid of me)

» leave school and get a full-time job

» leave home with the consent of Mum or Dad (Bovril would have to come too)

» choose my own doctor and decide on my own medical treatment

» have my own driving licence for moped or motorcycle (not that Mum would let me)

» buy a lottery ticket

» buy cigarettes (at least now it's legal)

» have sexual intercourse (mmmmmmh)

» get an abortion without Mum or Dad's consent (hope I won't ever need one)

» buy premium bonds (already got some from Aunty Jo)

» drink alcohol in a restaurant or hotel, but only if I'm having a meal (no drinking with Sal down the pub yet). But I still must have Mum or Dad with me if I'm interviewed by the police (not me!).

I've got to wait till I'm 17 before I can:

» gamble or go into a betting shop, but I can't make a bet till I'm 18

» join the armed forces, though Mum and Dad still have to approve

» get a regular driving licence for cars but not for heavy lorries

» go to prison.

But I'm jealous that Pete, this year, when he's 18, can:

» see an '18' film

» get a cheque book and credit card

» vote (maybe when I can vote, I'll help change the government)

>> apply for a mortgage

>> buy alcohol in a pub and drink it there

>> leave home, live with whoever he wants to, and get married without consent (won't be to Cilla, that's for sure, because she's gone off with David)

>> change his name without Mum and Dad's consent

>> see his birth certificate, even if he's adopted

>> be a member of a jury

>> get his own passport without Mum or Dad's signature.

**3rd January** Pete's sex mad. Seems to be already thinking of trying to put his 'medical knowledge' into practice. He's got a book out of the library about human behaviour. It has a bit about why people are attracted to one another. I'm sure it's all just about sex, but he says it's 'useful stuff' knowing how people choose mates. Useful for him, I reckon, given the problems he has.

He says it all happens by 'sexual sequencing'. When you meet someone at a party or something, whether you are first attracted to them or not probably just depends on looks and ways of dressing (but Pete says it's probably smells like pheromones as well). After that a kind of game begins which is stopped if one or the other person doesn't want to go on. Pete said the problem was when one person wanted to go on and the other didn't – like him and Cills.

His book says the 'courtship game' (sounds like something in ancient history) starts with looking at each other's bodies (the 'looking stage'), then gazing into each other's eyes. Then comes the 'talking stage', when you are finding out about one another; then a bit of touching, not the proper stuff but sort of disguised – helping you off with your coat, or taking your hand to help you across a road. Next, a bit more touching, like your bodies coming into closer contact, brushing against one another as if by accident. Things then get to a more intimate bit when you actually hold hands. Then comes the great leap to the kiss, followed by more serious touching and fumbling. Pete said I was too young to hear the next stages, as they were classified '18'. All sounds a bit too complicated for me. Why not just send them a text message saying 'Adctd 2 luvin U' – which means 'addicted to loving you', according to the other little book Pete gave me called *ltle bk of luv txt*.

Mum says Pete's got a one-track mind and that he ought to go and talk to the family doctor about it. Pete said, 'Hope she's got all afternoon'. I told Mum it was normal. *J-17* says the average male thinks of sex every 8 minutes, and I reckon with Pete it's every 8 seconds.

**4th January** Can't keep up. Pete's lost Cills and now fancies Sandy. But Sandy fancies Sam (who I reckon used to fancy me), so Pete's been trying to go out with Brenda, who will go out with anyone. However, Sam's going out with Giti, so Sandy's going for Rahul, who actually fancies Joanna.

I fancy Sam, and Pete says he likes me, but he never does anything about it. I am gasping to go out with him and he's on my mind all the time. I wish I could speak to him but I can't. Maybe I'll never find anyone to go out with and I'll die an old maid.

**5th January** Not a good way of starting the first weekend of the New Year – sitting here, fed up with work.

Pete's admitted to me he's tried the dreaded weed (I'm putting it in my blackmail book for when he gets narky). Said it was last year – with Cills. Asked him why it was OK to smoke cannabis but not cigarettes. He said maybe it wasn't all that OK. At the time he'd thought it was harmless, but he'd found out that smoking cannabis cigarettes had the same bad effects on your lungs as smoking normal cigarettes. He reckoned that what happened was that lots of teenagers started smoking the weed mixed with tobacco, and when they gave up the weed, they remained addicted to the tobacco and so kept on smoking. Hooked for a lifetime. Does he lose his money from Dad for not smoking cigarettes, though?

**6th January** Every time I sit down to start revising for my mock GCSEs, I get this awful sick feeling in my stomach and rush off to the toilet. Then I make myself a cup of coffee. How does Pete do it? His room looks and smells like the local council tip, his love life's a mess, his spots are like lunar craters and 10 times worse than mine, but he has got his work sorted. I just flit from book to book – from maths to biology, French to history, physics to English lit and lang – getting absolutely nothing done. At least I managed to finish some of the coursework. Mocks in 2 weeks – should have worked in the Christmas holidays like boring Mum kept on and on to me about. Don't know why it makes me furious, her always being right.

But anyhow, who works at Christmas? No way I'd miss the parties, plus everyone wanting presents which were 'just right'. Multicoloured boxer shorts from the Sock Shop for guess who (Sxx). Mum and Dad are the worst. It's 'anything you've made would be lovely'. Why can't they be the same as everybody else and like what I buy them? Got Dad a pair of boxer shorts too – really with-it. I found them in the Oxfam pile on New Year's Day (not sure what a Third World flood victim would make of them – use them for holding up his house maybe?). Bought some bright scarlet frilly knickers for Mum, to jazz up her sex life – but think Pete's now got them at the bottom of his wardrobe with his porno mags.

**7th January** Can't concentrate. My mind keeps coming back to everything I should be doing and can't – and Sam. I'm a world-class expert in excuses – got to message my friends to find out what they're doing, got to clean my room (even that's better than working), got to find my blue, crippled, 'chewed to nothing' pen. Worst thing is I've fallen out of love with Bovril. She shat on my bed last night – Mum made me clear it up, which made me puke.

Think I'll make a list of OK boys I know from school:

**John** – 8/10 – passable. Not a bad kisser (once at Christmas), lives three doors away, in my class, a bit young, still into Goth, think he dyes his hair, farts a lot – don't think I could live with so much smell.

**Sam** – 10/10 – desirable but doesn't seem to know I even exist. He's Pete's best friend, self-confident but not a poser. His dad's a leader too – a medical scientist – a geneticist or jeanome or something.

**Rahul** – 7/10 – Sita's older brother. Really attractive but a bit shy.

**Mark** – 2/10 – sad. Sixth-former and a total nerd – I'd rather go out with his 7-year-old brother.

**Andrew** – 5/10 – OK but in my year. Big-headed, tries it on with all the girls – even me. Smells of fags and wears white socks.

**Winston** – 8/10 – very fit and athletic and looks a bit like Prince William – yum, except even better-looking.

**Mike** – the midget. Nice, friendly but doesn't really score as he seems to prefer boys.

**8th January** Back at school. I never want to look at a French book again.

Resolution: not to be late any more.

Drama looks great. I'm acting being a paralysed girl after a car accident.

**9th January** Revision. It's no good. It won't go away. Kate's for coasting along and then slaving for 3 weeks before exams. She messaged saying '2 L8 anyway'. Can't muck about with GCSE, though – so much depends on the teacher's opinion.

Still hiding my last term's report from Mum and Dad. What was written is not brilliant, to say the least. Typical – Mum asked where it was. I said the school had decided not to give them out.

# REPORT

**English**

Not good — though she could be if she spent more time in class concentrating on her work and less talking to her friends. She also has irritating lapses of attention in class.

J. Jensen.

**Physics**

Oh dear — Susie not only doesn't do her own work properly but she distracts others as well. I have no idea whether she is any good at this subject. Her homework is always late and when it is handed in, it has more to do with flights of fancy than with fact. Having catpaw marks all over it doesn't help its legibility. O. Boil

**Biology**

Susie could do very well in her GCSE and might even manage an 'A'. However she must continue to work hard, right up to the examinations, to achieve this. She seems to have a particular interest in the workings of the human body. I wish her luck.

N. Smellie

**Chemistry**

Good at experimenting but not always with the ingredients she's meant to. V. Singh.

**French**

Susie can not keep up her interest in this subject. Her efforts to do absolutely nothing have paid off.

G. Dunlop

**History**

This is a confident, if rather over-gregarious young lady. Her essays, though informative, are rather slapdash. She needs to improve the organization of her study periods and homework. Recent history and discussion are her strong points. Trestring

**Maths**

Susie's performance is difficult to judge, as she has been away for a great many lessons this term. Much work is needed. When she is present, she tends to blow hot and cold, having periods of extreme activity followed by periods of quiet relaxation.

P. Pie.

**Drama**

She obviously enjoys the subject. Sometimes goes a bit 'over the top'. She should do well.

G. Smiles

**P.E.**

She has great ability but prefers not to use it.

K. Court

**Form Teacher's Report**

There are certainly some strengths here, and Susie is a most likeable person, BUT... she'll have to try harder. I think it would help if you would come and discuss this report with me please. Susie needs to improve her working methods if she is ever to succeed to the best of her abilities.

M. Rogers.

**Head's Report**

Patchy and rather disappointing. I feel that Susie could really do better. Her behaviour has not always been as good as it might have been either

I. MacIntosh

I think there must be a special book of *txt teacher's clichés* for use in school reports. It probably has translations as well, like:

'could do better if she tried' = 'totally hopeless'

'has great potential' = 'maybe but I've never seen it'

'outstanding work' = 'never turns up with homework'

'contributes well to discussions' = 'never stops talking'

'must beware of complacency' = 'bone idle'

'must apply herself better' = 'applying herself to work rather than flirting with every boy in sight might just help'.

Anyhow, I've decided I'm going to get French GCSE, become Prime Minister, and put the education system back together again – if there is a teacher left by then. Lucky about us having outside moderators, but I'm not sure how much it will help. Don't know whether schools are for passing exams, learning facts, keeping teachers off the streets, or for looking good in the school league tables. Private schools seem to win these anyhow – reckon they should, seeing that they are paid around £12,000 a year for each pupil.

**10th January** Even writing to smelly old Aunty Pam and embarrassing Uncle Bob is better than working. I put:

*Dear Aunty Pam and Uncle Bob*

*It was lovely seeing you at Christmas. Thank you for the lovely present and delicious lunch. The present was just what I wanted. How are you? I hope you are both well.*

*Thank you again...*

I make the perfect hypocrite, I reckon. Couldn't think of anything else. Certainly wasn't going to tell them about my non-existent social life. Couldn't even remember if they'd given me tights or a scarf – both DayGlo pink, which is what confused me. More for the Oxfam pile. There will be a very hot person in Africa wearing pink tights, a pink scarf, and boxer shorts with 'hard stuff' written across them. Bet Sam wouldn't fancy me if he saw me in DayGlo pink.

**11th January** Forgot what the homework was that had to be in tomorrow. Messaged all my friends. Panic made worse – they've all already done it. Kate and Sita had even gone off to the shops. Never asked me, did they? I just can't cope – but Mum said she'd help sort it out. Anyhow, Mary told me that John is going to chuck Kate. Says she's 'a slag'. He's one to talk.

Another thing I hate is favouritism from the teachers. I turn up in a mini-skirt and get 'Why are you wearing a postage stamp to school?'. Kate does the same and is praised for looking attractive.

List of birthday presents I'll leave around for everybody to see:

### Susie's Birthday List

* New body (top!) or brain – or just new clothes
* MP3 player
* Virgin music token (so I can buy my own CD and not one that Pete wants)
* Beatles CD
* New bike – given my parents never, ever, ever did give me the micro scooter I wanted so much
* Oil burner with cinnamon oil
* Obsession perfume
* Marc Chagall poster
* Hand-made clay Peruvian men
* Arty calendar
* Filofax organizer
* Nice ear-rings
* One-way ticket to Australia in case I fail my GCSEs
* Set of coloured covers for my mobile to match my clothes of the day

**12th January** Pete's in a sulk. Shouted at me for using the rest of his zit cream. Says he needs it more than me. Told him that men with pits on their face are great, and had he taken a close look at Prince William recently? Noticed Pete had this great graze on his cheek between the spots. He was furious I'd noticed. He and Sam had been riding Sam's new motorbike and had skidded on a bend. Luckily they'd been wearing crash helmets and the bike was only slightly bent. Pete said he'd kill me if I said anything to Mum or Dad.

**13th January** Mrs Smith, who lives two doors away, is giving me tips on how to sort out my work. Turns out she used to be a teacher. This week we're concentrating on:

## Organizing your room and your table

**1 MAKE SURE THE LIGHT IS RIGHT –**
*I'm to ask Mum to get me a new one that shines downwards.*

**2 CLEAR THE TABLE YOU USE AS A DESK –**
*This took ages, as I kept finding things that I thought I'd lost.*

**3 PUT ALL THE STUFF ON DIFFERENT SUBJECTS INTO SEPARATE, MARKED FILES –**
*Luckily Pete had some left over. He eventually managed to give me six. I sometimes think he doesn't want me to do well.*

**4 GET PAPER, PENS AND PENCILS –**
*Had these already but put them neatly together where I could find them.*

**5 GET RID OF DISTRACTIONS –**
*Mrs S said that music's OK – so have recorded the latest Robbie Williams album on my minidisc player.*

It's unbelievable – Mark (he only gets 1/10 now) is going out with a year 8 – baby-snatching. She's not only ugly with no sign of tits but is stupid as well. He's got no taste, which is why I don't fancy him. One thing about having a birthday and growing up – it makes you feel really embarrassed looking back at when you were 13 or 14. Especially reading my old diaries (the ones Pete read – kill, kill). I can't believe the things I wrote. Absolutely cringe at what I wore, who I fancied, and who was my idol.

# All About **Me**

**2**

18 Clifton Road
Hawsley, Londres
Angleterre
15th January

Dear Marie Cerveau,

I am writing to you because mon school says you are my Exchange Français. Je hope to arrive this summer par train via le Channel Tunnel, n'est ce pas? Avez vous peur de travelling dans un tunnel sub la mer?

I thought peut etre vous might like to know quelque chose about moi and my famille. I hope you will write and tell me quelque chose about you.

Ma nom is Susie. J'ai nearly 16 years et my birthday est January 16th. Mes eyes sont grey/brown et ma hair est long et aussi brownish. Je n'aime pas school much because je think the teachers sont boring but je ne suis pas mal at biology and pas assez good at French.

## PLAN OF MA FAMILLE

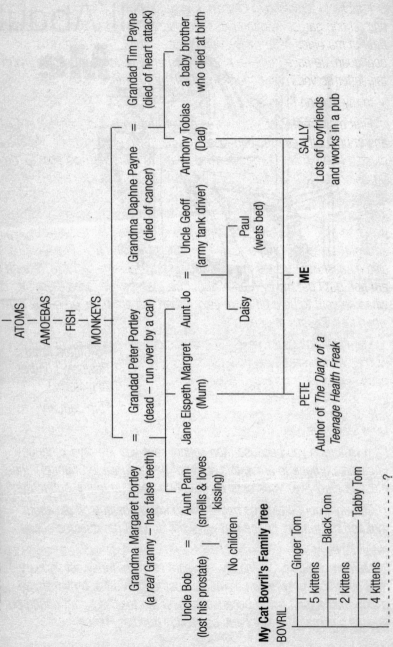

ADAM & EVE + SNAKE + APPLE
ATOMS
AMOEBAS
FISH
MONKEYS

Grandad Tim Payne (died of heart attack)

Grandma Daphne Payne (died of cancer)

a baby brother who died at birth

Anthony Tobias (Dad)

Uncle Geoff (army tank driver)

Grandad Peter Portley (dead – run over by a car)

Jane Elspeth Margret (Mum)

Aunt Jo

SALLY
Lots of boyfriends and works in a pub

Paul (wets bed)

Daisy

ME

Grandma Margaret Portley (a *real* Granny – has false teeth)

Aunt Pam (smells & loves kissing)

Uncle Bob (lost his prostate)

No children

PETE
Author of *The Diary of a Teenage Health Freak*

**My Cat Bovril's Family Tree**

BOVRIL
Ginger Tom
— 5 kittens
Black Tom
— 2 kittens
Tabby Tom
— 4 kittens
?

14

*I habite in a maison in London. It is ne pas very jolie. But I love it and it has un bon garden. Ma famille is mon père, ma mère, mon older brother Pete et ma older sister Sally et une chat – Bovril. J'aime my chat beaucoup. Je have done un plan of my family which I am sending with this letter so vous can understand my family better.*

*In my maison there are:*

*First mon frère Pete who is très clever and un grand pain. He is 17 ans et un 'boff', and toujours gets le 'A\*'s in his examinations. He has un place a Nottingham University to do medicin. He is learning how to 'drive' un voiture but is très mal at that. He is aussi un 'Health Freak' and pense toujours of his body. I think qu'il est un hypochondriac. Do you have these in France too? He is also always trying to get off with les girls but is not very bon at it. He has un très joli ami who is called Sam, who all the girls aiment beaucoup et me also, but he just thinks of me as Pete's petite sister. Aussi Pete teases me all the time and calls me 'stupide' though I am not, but I get my own back about his glasses. He takes them off when he veut to be a bit more sexy. When you are here, prenez le care when he takes his glasses off!*

*Ma sister Sally a 21 years. She is très difficile et une rebel. Mum worries about elle all the time. She habite with her latest boyfriend, who nobody here aimes much. Elle est très, très, très pretty and I wish I looked like her. She goes to beaucoup de parties and spends tout her time at le pub where she works. She used to be a chevaux (hair) dresser.*

*Mon père has a gros stomach and is almost bald. He is gentil but his travail is not very gentil. He is a 'Killer de Pestes'. Il s'appelle Tony et il smokes cigarettes and pretends il doesn't.*

*Next is ma mère. She is très bossy and interfering but I think you will really aime her because she is très jolie and funny. Elle eats too much and aime beaucoup le chocolat. Elle s'appelle Jane et elle est a bit grosse everywhere but pretends she isn't. I worry about getting grosse like her.*

*She always wants to know quelque chose about what I am doing and where I am going and avec who. Sometimes she has the same colour hair as moi but it's curly.*

*Je want to visite Disneyland Paris, but ma mère ne want pas me to, parce ce que elle thinks that I will not learn beaucoup de French there and elle n'aime pas Monsieur Mickey Mouse.*

*Mes amies are Kate, Rachel, Emma, Sita, and sometimes Mary. Le music que nous aimons beaucoup is Robbie Williams, David Gray, Travis (j'ai have a minidisc player and un mobile). We aime going 'clubbing' (mais ma mère ne know pas about this). My plus close friend who really understands me is Bovril – ma chat – who also aime les boys très much and is always avec them and having kittens. Moi aimes les boys aussie but I don't have le boyfriend a ce moment.*

*J'aime les sports, comme swimming and running, and je suis in the school team, but also j'ai hayfever. I hate ma face as it keeps getting les spots and I have to cover it with le make-up.*

*Quelque chose else about me? J'aime le shopping, je n'aime pas global warming, or le hunting of animals. J'ai have had my ears pierced but wanted to have my tongue pierced mais ma mere wouldn't let me. J'ai have visited Paris once before quand my papa won some money on le lottery Anglais.*

*I hope you like my French – please write about yourself and what 'group' you like beaucoup. Do you keep a diary? Je keep a très special book into which I stick everything.*

*Your exchange amie,*

*Susie*

*P.S. Je n'aime pas meat, and when I come and stay with you can I just mange vegetables please? Je pense that it is cruel and horrid to kill les animals.*

*P.P.S. Joke:*
*Question: Why does mon frère Pete, who finds his body si intéressant, wear his underpants in the shower?*
*Answer: Because il n'aime pas regarder le unemployed.*

# Sweet **Sixteen** and Never Been ...

**16th January** MY BIRTHDAY!

MY BIRTHDAY!!

MY BIRTHDAY!!

MY BIRTHDAY!!!

MY BIRTHDAY!!!!

MY BIRTHDAY!!!!!

Pete's first words to me were 'Just cos you've reached the age of consent doesn't mean you've got to say yes to sex'. Sam won't remember. He's still going out with Giti. I pretend I don't mind because I really like her, but it actually makes me totally miserable. Nobody remembers Christmas and birthdays if they come together. Mum and Dad could have been a bit more thoughtful when they decided to have me in the first place.

Some of the time Mum really does my head in – fuss, fuss, fuss – but sometimes she's wonderful. Gave me a 'surprise' tea party. Kate, Sita and Emma all came round. Why couldn't Pete have invited Sam? He invited Randy Joe instead. Even Sally came – skived off work. I'm sure she'll get the sack. Miss her not being at home so I can talk to her about things.

**My presents** ✳✳✳✳✳✳✳✳✳✳✳✳✳✳✳✳✳✳✳✳✳✳✳

**Mum** – new body (but no new brain) and a Heath Ledger poster – brilliant

**Dad** – second-hand bike to replace the one stolen last month (not surprising as I was riding his all the time), plus a crash helmet which I could have done without

**Pete** – forgot again – that makes six birthdays and four Christmases in a row. So he promised to get me a National Lottery ticket. Told him I wanted 01 02 03 04 05 06

**Sal** – make-up paintbox (slightly used?), perfume and an invite to the pub

**Emma** – three 'txt messaging' books

**Kate** – compilation tape she made up herself – can't wait to see what's on it

**Sita** – Indian ear-rings – OK!

**Randy Joe** – forgot, though I suspect it was him who donated a couple of gas releases during tea

**Bovril** – think she's been at it again, so it will have to be kittens…again!

**17th January** Email from Rani, who used to be in my class at school. We competed against one another in running – till her dad got a job in Birmingham.

My emailed reply!

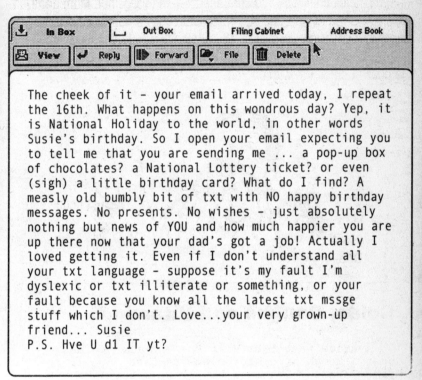

| ⬇ **In Box** | ☐ **Out Box** | **Filing Cabinet** | **Address Book** |

| 📧 **View** | ↩ **Reply** | ➦ **Forward** | 📨 **File** | 🗑 **Delete** |

The cheek of it - your email arrived today, I repeat
the 16th. What happens on this wondrous day? Yep, it
is National Holiday to the world, in other words
Susie's birthday. So I open your email expecting you
to tell me that you are sending me ... a pop-up box
of chocolates? a National Lottery ticket? or even
(sigh) a little birthday card? What do I find? A
measly old bumbly bit of txt with NO happy birthday
messages. No presents. No wishes - just absolutely
nothing but news of YOU and how much happier you are
up there now that your dad's got a job! Actually I
loved getting it. Even if I don't understand all
your txt language - suppose it's my fault I'm
dyslexic or txt illiterate or something, or your
fault because you know all the latest txt mssge
stuff which I don't. Love...your very grown-up
friend... Susie
P.S. Hve U d1 IT yt?

**18th January** Pete's pathetic – a tiny cold and he thinks he's dying. Moan, moan, moan. But as soon as Mum told him there was a letter for him, he leapt out of bed and rushed downstairs. Letter was from the library – saying he'd 3 books which were overdue by a month. I nearly fell downstairs laughing. Pete says I'm basically an unsympathetic person and that I never believe him when he says he's ill; and if I want any sympathy when I get ill, I'd better not expect it from him. Told him everybody gets colds and nobody knows anything about them. Nobody but Dr Pete Payne, BMKA (Bloody Medical Know All), that is.

Even if he had yesterday off, he hadn't wasted his time. He's written an article for the school newspaper where he's doing a weekly column on health. This week, it's all about his own health problem – 'Colds'. Next week it's going to be on 'Hayfever' (my problem), then skin problems, asthma, headaches, sex and contraception, throwing-up and the runs. He's asked me to write the one on sex and contraception, as he thought I ought to learn about it now I'm 16, if I didn't know it all already. He gave me his 'Colds' piece to read as an example of the kind of thing he wants. He doesn't credit me with a mind.

# Colds, Coughs and Vitamin C

On average we get between one and five colds a year, though my sister seems to have one all the time. (She claims it's hayfever, which I have to agree is caused by something different.)

Colds are caused by viruses called Rhino viruses (Rhino meaning nose or nostril, like rhinoceroses, which are named after their big horns). There are loads of different types of these viruses and our bodies are not much good at fighting them off, which is why we get loads of colds.

These viruses are spread in the sprays from our coughs and sneezes more than by poking our fingers up our noses to get at our snot. (You still shouldn't do that, or at least not where your friends can see, and as for eating it afterwards – a disgusting habit, even if it does taste good, but don't ask me how I know.)

So why do all us horrible people get snotty and drippy when we have a cold? Well, there are these tiny glands in our noses which make the sticky stuff that mixes with all the nasty things that get up our noses – like our fingers, dust, other dirt, and bacteria – to make up our very own personal snot. All this then gets mixed up with our nose hairs (yes, we all have them, not just those wrinklies out there – though theirs are more obvious and foul).

This lovely mixture of viruses, snot and so on stirs everything up, and what with blowing your nose – no, sorry, forget that – wiping your nose on your sleeve, or sniffing and swallowing the gunk, everything around and in your nose gets nicely red and sore.

Another fact: although colds are commoner in the winter, just getting cold doesn't seem to make you more likely to get 'a cold'. That's what the research shows anyway. It also shows that kissing someone with a cold doesn't mean that the other person will get a cold, as long as the one with the cold doesn't breathe or sneeze – so keep up the good work, all you snoggers out there (and practise kissing without breathing!).

Because they are caused by viruses, antibiotics don't do anything towards curing colds, so it's probably better just to use something that makes you 'feel' better, like paracetamol, hot drinks, and tender loving care from someone who loves you, should you be so lucky (definitely not my sister).

Although drug companies spend millions of pounds trying to advertise 'cold cures', there is nothing that 'cures' colds, although something to dry up your snot may make you feel happier.

And as for Vitamin C, well, you can try it, even if none of the experiments so far show that it actually works.

I'll never forgive him – telling the whole school. I threw his mug of last week's coffee at him, where he'd been growing new and disgusting strains of fungal penicillin on – and yelled that it was him who said it wouldn't make any difference to his cold – getting soaking wet and having antibiotics. Dad was furious about the coffee stain, because it did make a difference to the carpet.

Anyhow, I was interested in what he said about Vitamin C. We'd just done that in school and I thought it cured something called 'scurvy', when your gums bleed and your teeth all drop out. Mrs Smellie said they'd done an experiment on sailors with scurvy in the 18th century and had tried giving different groups of sailors cider, sulphuric acid, vinegar, sea water, mustard, two oranges and two lemons, and a ship's normal diet. We were being taught about 'controls', and the question was whether this was a controlled experiment. I said no, but Pete said that I'd got it wrong – the ship's normal diet was the 'control'. He explained that without having one group of sailors who didn't have anything extra, they wouldn't have been able to tell whether the sailors had just got better with time alone. Anyhow, this experiment showed that the sailors who had the oranges and lemons got better and the sailors who had the other things or nothing didn't. It wasn't until a hundred years later that they found out it was Vitamin C in the oranges and lemons that had done it. Maybe Vitamin C will be found to stop colds in another hundred years.

**19th January** Mocks have started – no comment.

**20th January** Mum has had a nightmare that the librarians from the local library are out to kill her. She dreamt they were stationed with guns at every window and door of the house, with no escape. They were chanting 'bring back the books, bring back the books' and 'pay your fines, pay your fines'. No more driving lessons till Pete takes his books back. Mum thinks it's really mean on the other people wanting the books. Pete said he'd return the books but dream interpretation was rubbish. He'd had a dream about being chased while naked and riding a burning horse down a long corridor full of people.

Makes me almost believe that dreams are kinds of messages – I'm sometimes dreaming about a fire engine when I'm woken up by my alarm bell. No one seems to know whether dreams are just a waste-disposal machine for unwanted thoughts, or whether they are DEEPLY meaningful. One of Pete's unreturned books was on the interpretation of dreams. It fell open at the appropriate page, so he must have been reading it.

**Being chased** – dreamers want to escape from someone. The person chasing them can also represent some aspect of the dreamer that they are unhappy with.

**Riding** – a fairly obvious sexual symbol, though it commonly represents fear as well as desire.

**Nakedness** – depending on circumstances, and on whether the dreamers are embarrassed and the crowd takes any notice, this can mean inferiority, inadequacy or, alternatively, a desire to be different.

**Fire** – means passion and danger, and often that thoughts about sex are causing trouble.

**Corridor** – a feeling that you want to return to your mother's womb and security.

Pete's sure got problems, but it seems to me that you can interpret dreams any way you want to, like the stars.

**23rd January** Speechless – FIVE of my national lottery numbers came up! There it was in the paper! I'd won £100,000! More money than I'd ever dreamed of. I could get all the birthday presents I missed out on, plus a stereo hi-fi, an MP3 stick and a ticket to Australia!

I pitched into Pete's room without knocking. He did not look pleased. 'My ticket, my ticket – give it me, give it me – I've won,' I screamed. Blank puzzled stare. 'What are you talking about?' I could only scream 'My ticket, my ticket', on and on and on.

The bastard hadn't even bought it. I held his pillow over his face, but he was too strong…so just sobbed and sobbed.

Louise was doing art, though now maybe she's not. She's having second thoughts as she was crucified by Mrs Saicops, her art teacher. Sometimes teachers can be really cruel. She said that some pupils have application and no talent but that Louise has neither application nor talent. I think this is shitty and not even true. It's straight-up bitchiness because Mrs Saicops doesn't like Louise. No knowledge of psychology, these teachers. If I'm told I'm bad at something, it makes me mad, and I become bad at it so as to fit in with what the teachers think.

Teachers bullying are bad enough – other kids even worse. Some people seem to attract it, especially those who don't know how to stick up for themselves. We talked about it on the school council and we're drawing up a code to try to stop it. Sometimes it's just people being rude to one another, like saying 'Your mum's a tart, I wouldn't fancy sleeping with her', and at other times it's real physical stuff, with several boys picking on one who sticks out.

Still can't believe about the lottery ticket. Some people go mad when they think they've won and they haven't – why did I trust Pete?

# 4 My **Writes**
and
**Animal Rights**

**27th January** Louise's dad had it out with Mrs Saicops about her art. Glad it wasn't my dad. I'd be acutely grieved – but it worked. Mrs Saicops praised her last life drawing – creep.

Dad kept asking me questions about my life, just as all Pete's friends were arriving to watch the big match. Mark and Sam came with Randy Joe. Dad talked but I didn't listen and he left in a strop!

I changed into Miss Sixties and my new crop top. It's a bit clingy and revealing, so I changed out again. Can't see myself wearing it in public – despite Mum nagging I've never worn it.

Football's boring – I don't know who anyone is…except for Beckham and Owen. Wrongly thought I was supporting Sam's team. Made some remarks about Joanna – which certainly weren't all nice, but weren't all nasty. One advantage of older brothers – they do have friends.

**29th January** Mocks have finished – still no comment!

**3rd February** Note from Mrs Smith about keeping up with my work plans, so I've got to work.

ORGANIZING YOUR SUBJECTS

1 Write a list of all the subjects you are doing.

2 List them from the ones that you know least about to the ones you know best.

3 Then list for each subject all the bits of that subject you should know.

4 Keep each subject in its folder to stop them from getting muddled up.

5 Get a diary and work out how many days and hours you have for revision before the exams.

6 Work out how much time you have to revise each subject (using simple division!) and write out a programme of work covering all the subjects equally.

7 When you are revising, choose some topics which you already know well and some that you don't, so that you keep feeling OK about it and don't panic or get depressed.

Afraid in my list everything should be top. I'm trying to stop myself panicking, so here goes:

MATHS (no comment)

FRENCH ('orrible)

COMBINED SCIENCE (no comment)

PHYSICS (great but difficult, and awful teacher)

CHEMISTRY (the sexual kind – preferably)

BIOLOGY (the real facts!)

ENGLISH (sort of OK)
ENGLISH LIT (OK)
HISTORY (more OK)
DRAMA (comes naturally to me)

Texted it to my friend Kate – but reckon she's hard at it because there was no reply.

Fed up with work, there must be more to life than this. But Mrs Smith says 'the more you can do today, the less you need to do tomorrow' – and that working will make me feel less anxious.

Can't find my French book – not that I really looked. My biology list looks like this:

*Life Classifications, Bacteria and Viruses, Fungi, Foods and Feeding.*

*Green Plant Nutrition, Animal Nutrition, Water Uptake, Blood and Lymphatic System, Respiration, Excretion.*

*Temperature Regulation, Sensitivity, Co-ordination and Response, Support and Locomotion, Reproduction: Plants and Humans, Genes, Evolution, Ecology.*

Doesn't seem so bad written out like this. Eighteen topics, say two hours for each. Almost seems possible.

**4th February** Want a Valentine's Day party. No chance of Mum saying yes – not after Sally's 'breaking-up' party 5 years ago, where everything got broken up!

How does Mum do it? She always knows when I'm lying. Asked me whether Kate and me had been smoking in my room. I said, 'Of course not, Mum. Why do you always pick on me?' On and on. 'Don't lie to me –

I know you have, haven't you?' 'No, honest Mum, it wasn't me.' Perhaps it was the smell (even through all those joss sticks?). She's like a firework – we'd just lit up and – bang! – she appeared out of nowhere.

Gave me the same old lecture. I know it's wrong – she doesn't have to tell me. And it doesn't help, her telling me again and again that the number of people dying from the effects of smoking is the equivalent of a jumbo jet crashing every day. That it's not just lung cancer that it causes, but heart disease and bronchitis. That once you've started, it's much more difficult to stop. I'm not interested in what's going to happen to me when I'm an old hag in 50 years' time. Anyhow I don't smoke often, and I'm not going to get addicted, and I wouldn't dream of smoking if I was pregnant. No way I'd want to harm my baby. (Not that I'm going to GET pregnant – I don't even have a boyfriend to try with!)

**5th February** Pete wants Bov to be in an animal experiment. He saw this TV programme about a link between two parts of the brain that gives us our sex drive. Seeing Bov at it all the time, he said she'd be ideal to experiment on and for him to look inside her brain.

I do think it's cruel to do animal experiments, particularly on Bov – after all, she must have feelings. Discussed it with Bov, who wasn't much help. I was thinking of joining an 'Anti Experiments on Animals' group in the 'Animal Rights' phase of my life when I was 14, but never did because they were so cruel to human beings. They said there was no point in testing drugs on animals because humans are different from animals, and some drugs tested OK on animals have been shown to be not safe for humans. As for using animals for making and testing cosmetics – just so you can look beautiful. Specially as all those poor animals had such a hard time with BSE and foot and mouth and all.

It's so annoying arguing with Pete as he's brilliant at it and always seems to be right. I know many of the points I make are correct but the words just don't come out right. He says I'm only giving a bit of the argument. There have been experiments on animals to do with drugs that are saving lots of lives – though Pete agrees that making calves live in crates to make them taste better isn't good.

But animal experiments were essential in the development of the vaccine which means there is no more smallpox in the world. They were also vital in the development of penicillin and insulin (the medicine used by people with diabetes), and the drugs used to cure childhood leukaemia. Pete had lots more examples, but I didn't want to hear them. He'd persuaded me that if the experiments are carefully carried out so as to cause as little suffering as possible, then it's OK. I wanted to know how come there was all this fuss about people living near power lines and how it might be bad for them, but it didn't seem to matter having animals wandering around in fields with power lines running over them. Pete said that there was no proof that it was bad for humans or for animals, though he did wonder whether we should be giving rabbits mobiles to see whether they ended up with brain tumours.

We both agreed that setting fire to people's houses because they are involved in animal experiments is mental, and it's also plain disgusting for girls to plaster their faces with animal products.

At the hairdresser's I asked the lady whether the stuff she was washing my hair with had been tested on an animal. She said she'd shampooed her cat with it and it seemed OK. Wasn't quite what I'd meant. Maybe the cat was OK afterwards, but I was a mess.

**8th February** At last – my French Exchange has written back. Not that she said much. Her letter was rather formal: 'Thank you for your letter. I'll tell you all about myself when you come to Paris. See you soon, Marie Cerveau.' Wonder if I can txt her but she didn't say whether she was mobiled.

At last, a birthday present from Pete: a white rabbit with pink eyes. Had they been experimenting on it, putting drops in its eyes? Turned out it was just a pinked-eyed rabbit – how was I to know? Pete was given it by Sam, who was given it by his dad, who had rescued it from being experimented on. Thought of calling it 'Sam', but settled for 'Pinko'. Mum's furious. Says it's going to be her who has to clean it out and feed it, and look after it when it's sick. Don't actually like it much. Don't fancy its pathetic pink eyes staring at me all the time.

**9th February** NOBODY, NOBODY noticed my new haircut. Wasted £29.

Started revising BACTERIA AND VIRUSES. To help me remember, I made lots of little notes and stuck them all over the house, above my bed, in the toilet, on the back of the hall door.

**Rubella:**

1 *Also known as German measles*
2 *Caused by a virus*
3 *Harmless to person who catches it*
4 *Very harmful to baby if you catch it when you are pregnant*
5 *Can be prevented by having an immunization against it*
6 *Everyone should be immunized, when they are 1 year old.*

**Chlamydia:**

1 *Caused by a bacteria*
2 *Gives a discharge from the penis or vagina, pain on peeing, but sometimes no symptoms at all in the early stages*
3 *Can make you sterile (not able to have babies)*
4 *Easily treated with an antibiotic*
5 *Quite common in men and women*
6 *The commonest sexually transmitted infection in young people*
7 *Condoms reduce the chances of catching it.*

Pete stuck up a notice saying 'If you think you've got a sexually transmitted disease, Chlamydia or any other, your local GU (Genito-Urinary) clinic number is.........'. Mum went spare – notes about French verbs all over the house is one thing, notes about sexually transmitted diseases is another: wasn't having her house turned into a public toilet, thank you.

Pete's in Mum's bad books anyway. He missed a driving lesson last night – the last one before his test. I made things better by telling Mum how many people had probably survived as a result. Pete's not amused. He thinks I'm joking, but while he's learning, I'm on the most efficient but dangerous form of transport known – my bike.

I remember when Pete had his accident a couple of years ago. He had a long lecture from the doctor about how 200 people a year get killed and 24,000 injured on bikes each year, and saying that cycle and motorcycle accidents are the commonest cause of death in young people.

Pete's never worn a crash helmet since, and neither have I, but we both know we should. I'd look such a nerd with Dad's white plastic bowl of a birthday present on my head. If there was a law, then I'd have to wear one, and so would everyone else, and we'd all look nerds and wouldn't stand out.

**10th February** Got my own passport from the post office today. Ghastly photo – makes me look like Dad. Now I know I'm not adopted.

# Broken **Hearts** and Broken **Families**

**12th February** Pete failed his driving test today. Damaged his sensitive ego, especially as Sam's passed (great). Also Pete managed to damage his driving instructor's car.

We're about to have a German invasion. Uncle Geoff, who's married to Aunty Jo (Mum's sister who doesn't smell), has gone off with 'another younger woman'. Aunty Jo can't stand being by herself any longer, so she's coming to stay, with her two children, Daisy and Paul, so she can get a bit of sympathy from Mum. Can't see why anyone would go off with an alcoholic, curly-headed, midget ex-British Army tank driver like Uncle Geoff. Would have to be even more desperate than me – though Pete thinks that even I won't have any trouble finding a boy. There are 3 per cent more boys than girls around nowadays, and by the year 2025 there will be 105 men to every 100 women.

If Dad left Mum for another woman, Pete said he'd go to the trouble of doing him over.

It's quite out of order – I have to share my bedroom with my cousin Daisy. I know I don't particularly like the name 'Susie' – but Daisy! Daisy was a 9-year-old brat the last time I saw her. I hated her, and her 5-year-old brother, Paul, who used to wet his bed. Always knew because he never got up in the same coloured pyjamas as he went to bed in. Mum said his bed-wetting was because his bladder wasn't mature yet. Like the rest of him, I'd say. He'd got better with some kind of alarm thing in his bed that woke him up when he peed. He used to tell Pete how he'd dream about wanting to pee in his sleep, and then he'd wake up and find he'd done it in his bed. Got my own back on Mum about not being able to use the phone. She's on to her sister in Germany every day. One day Uncle Geoff's gone, the next he's back.

Couldn't bear it if Mum and Dad separated. Suppose you never know though. Even celebs like Kidman and Cruise and now Kate Winslet are doing it and their kids look absolutely miserable. I'm sure that I'll never get divorced – doubt whether I'll even get the chance. If it did happen to Mum and Dad, I don't think I would be able to speak about it. Hardest thing would be deciding who to go with. I wouldn't want to hurt either of them and make them think I didn't love them as much. Would be specially bad at celebrations like Christmas and things – having to choose. Some things might be better, like I could get twice as much pocket-money. Also I could be with Dad when I wanted to stay out late and didn't want to be hassled about work, and with Mum when I wanted money for clothes. (Dad still can't see why I can't make do with Sal's old clothes. Can't expect him to know anything about 'fashion' in his old M & S suit bought by Mum.)

Kate's parents divorced when she was 4. She couldn't understand why her father went. She's never really forgiven him for what he did to her mum. It was dreadful. Grown-ups are really inconsiderate and selfish. They just think of themselves. But actually I can't imagine myself ever finding someone I'd want to spend all my life with. Certainly no one I know now – not even Sam. Kate stayed with her mum, living off social security, and they are always short of money. She doesn't think people understand how bad it is for the children. One in three marriages ends in divorce. It was when Kate went through a bad patch at school recently that she felt she needed her dad most. Come to think of it, Eddie, a friend of Pete's who came on holiday with us a few years ago – his parents are divorced too, and his Dad is in Jamaica, so he hardly ever sees him. But he seems OK about it.

**13th February** Don't feel like writing today. Totally PISSED OFF.

**14th February** VALENTINE'S DAY. NO PARTY, NO CARDS, NO RED ROSES.

My Valentine's Day has been as romantic as a day's outing to Aunty Pam's.

Pete got 2 cards which he waved under my nose when I got home, along with 3 txt messages and an email card. Did get one of those myself, which said 'Gna Mak U An Ofr U Cnt Rfs'. Had a block on who it came from, though Pete said I could have one of his cards second-hand

if I wanted. I asked him where his fatal charm comes from – with his pebble eyes. Never see it myself. He probably wrote them all himself. Did my moan bit to Mum about having a party. Think maybe she's cracking.

**15th February** Two day-late Valentine cards! One's definitely from Mum. Can tell from the innocent smile on her face and the exclamations of 'I wonder who it can be from?' and (from Dad) 'Who's the secret admirer then?'. The other one – I hope it's Sam, it must be Sam, let it be Sam. Sam, Sam, is it you?

**16th February** It was Sam – Pete made him do it. Totally embarrassed.

**19th February** A week off school.

**20th February** Daisy and her brother Paul arrive tomorrow – yugh. What a way to spend half-term. Lecture from Mum about being 'nice to your poor cousins'. Lecture from Pete about girls being stupider than boys because more of them are smoking nowadays and anyway they have smaller brains. Told him it is quality not quantity that counts.

**21st February** Am writing this sitting on the toilet. Nowhere else in our house is private. Daisy doesn't seem very upset to me. Just interested in commenting on everything in my room.

**22nd February** Daisy's a pain. Must be awful for her, but it's tough always being nice to someone you don't like, even if they are having a hard time. She hasn't improved since I last saw her. Aunty Jo's really nice. She's in Sal's old room. Daisy and the thing called her brother must have their father's PPP (Pissing, Poor, Protoplasmic) genes. My biology revision has not been in vain. I also got an A – for my test on bacteria.

Paul's sleeping in Pete's room. Pete is none too pleased, especially as Paul wet the bed last night. Just got up and turned the mattress over to try and hide it. Couldn't hide the smell though.

Got it from Mum that Paul's bed-wetting had started again when his Dad left. This didn't impress Pete, who said he'd go and live at Sam's if it went on. I offered to go instead. Pete said no way would Sam be interested in MY body. Mum said she hoped there's no way Sam would be interested in Pete's. Pete was not amused. Seems to have lost his sense of humour. Mum said later that all boys worried about being homosexual sometime. I think he's depressed – as Brenda's not responding to his charms and is not impressed by him failing his driving test.

Pete likes teasing as long as it's not him being teased. When Mum asked him if he wanted anything from Sainsbury's, he said 'Yes – some sanity please'. Bov's the only one who understands how I feel about S. If Mum and Dad separated, I'd take Bov – whoever I went with.

**23rd February** It's like old times. Rani's down from Birmingham for the day. It's her half-term too. Great to see her and catch up. Bit strange at first, though, seeing if we were the same people as before. Luckily she seemed to get on with Daisy OK. She wanted to know if Daisy missed her friends, specially at times like half-term. Daisy said 'yes' – but that it would be difficult telling them about what had happened, even though a lot of their parents were divorced too. They'd moved around a lot because of her dad's job in the army, which made it difficult to keep friends. But Germany, where her dad was stationed now, was just like England – same shops and everything. And everyone spoke English.

Her dad was very strict when he was at home – which wasn't often. Daisy's sure her mum only married her dad because she was pregnant with her. Sometimes she even wonders whether he really is her dad. Now he's gone off with her mum's best friend, Daisy's pleased that she's with her mum, but she was really angry with her mum and dad for not telling her or Paul anything about what was going on.

**24th February** Daisy keeps a diary too! Found me writing mine – I forgot to lock the lav door while peeing and writing. Perhaps I'll get a bit of peace when I go off to Paris.

Big mistake! Gave Mum something I found about 'Having a Party' in a women's magazine Aunty Jo bought. Wanted to keep the pressure up.

# Having a Party

* Limit the numbers you invite by insisting it's by 'invitation only'. Print out the invitations on a computer. Make them instantly recognizable and difficult to copy.

* Take everything down – pictures, and so on. If something can be broken, it will be. Also allow for the fact that the house WILL BE a total wreck afterwards. Cigarette ends get everywhere, as do the pull fasteners to beer cans, and empty beer cans. Even six months later you may still be finding half bottles of whisky stuffed down the back of the sofa. Leave the whole of the next day for clearing up – not just a few hours in the morning. Try arranging for a few hard workers to stay overnight to clean up, but limit numbers to those who are useful.

* Arrange for a couple of boys to be bouncers and pay them to drink milk all evening. They can keep away gatecrashers. (Gatecrashers are the worst menace –

your friends will at least feel faintly ashamed at smashing everything up – gatecrashers feel nothing.) Get the bouncers to throw drunks out before they puke over everything. As back-up – have a parent or some other adult in the house (but not at the party) to help you if things get out of hand.

* Never, never have any of your parents' drink around in the fridge or anywhere else – it will get stolen. It's too embarrassing to search people for hard liquor on the way in, so ask them not to bring it. Get them to stick to wine or beer. Try getting your parents and friends to help out with the costs. Wine is preferred and mixing drinks is disastrous. Never have a 'punch' – people will lace it with everything and you'll need to hire an ambulance as well as bouncers.

* Have lots of food – it helps mop up the alcohol. But most people will probably have eaten beforehand. Have things to eat which don't make too much mess. Always have everything disposable – cups, plates, and so on. Have lots of dustbin bags around.

* If you smell cannabis, get the smokers outside onto neutral ground and only allow them back in after they've stopped smoking (thus at least avoiding YOU getting involved with the law). Try having different things going on in different rooms – music, videos, dancing, kissing. Music really matters – so it must be good. Try checking out people's tastes beforehand or get them to bring their favourite discs.

* Remember – as host you may have a difficult time at your own party, but it is a long-term investment. Lots and lots of invitations to other people's parties in exchange for short-term hell.

Mum read it and said 'I'll think about it …' I know 'I'll think about it' equals 'No!'

**25th February** Pete's turned into a goody-goody. He's just trying to impress – but who cares? He said why didn't I write one of my problem page letters to help Daisy, like I'd written to *Teenage Weekly* about being fat. Anyhow Daisy and I wrote it together.

*Dear Editor,*

*I am very depressed and lonely. I thought that my mum and dad were happily married. About a year ago they started arguing and shouting at one another. Dad's gone off with Mum's best friend and I never see him. If Dad can go off, I'm afraid that Mum may leave too – and I don't know what will happen to me and my brother. Nobody tells us anything. Daisy – aged 12.*

Back to b\*\*\*y school tomorrow. But a relief to escape Daisy.

**3rd March** Pete's now Macho Hero Number One in Daisy's eyes – she thinks he's 'WUUUNDERFUL'. The letter that Daisy and I had written to *Teenage Weekly*, and a reply, were published.

'It may help you to know you're not alone – so try talking to your friends about it. Each year in the UK there are around 175,000 divorces. For every two marriages, there is now one divorce. In fact, one in five 16-year-olds have parents who are divorced. In spite of this, a huge study of young people showed that they themselves are very optimistic about marriage, and that 29 out of every 30 wanted to get married and 24 out of every 25 wanted to have children. One reason for the increase in divorce might be because in previous centuries people lived much shorter lives and would usually have been married for only 20 years or less. Nowadays, with people living to over 70, you may have 50 years or more of married life. No one would pretend that being together for all this time is easy, and most couples will have some arguments and disagreements from time to time.

Other common reasons for parents splitting up are changes in the way people feel about themselves, and changes in their attitudes and in what they mind strongly about. Sometimes people behave in an unacceptable way (sexually or with violence) to the other person, or are unable to cope with children; or they have money problems.

It is very rare for children to want their parents to split up, even if this means the end of arguments and shouting. Therefore almost all children feel sad, and sometimes become bitter and angry with the remaining parent. As parents are caught up in their own anger and upset feelings, the children often feel left out and lonely, and in spite of the fact that it is not their fault at all, they may also feel that they are in some way responsible for the break-up.

Try telling your parents that you need to talk to them about what is going on and what is going to happen: where you are going to live, who you are going to live with, what school you are going to go to, where the absent parent is going to live. What young people don't want is responsibility for making any of the decisions – like which parent they want to stay with.

One of the best things for separating parents to do is to continue to talk to one another and to their children. They must also realize that their children will continue to love them both, and will want to be reassured of the love of both.

We thought you might like to read about the feelings of some of the other people who have written to us about the same problem.'

---

*'The thing I am most upset about is my mum leaving when I was only 2. Now I am 10 and I'm going through a bad patch at home and school at the moment and it is at times like these that I need my mum badly. My dad is very good, but I did need my mum a while back because I started having fits. I think my dad misses mum as well but he doesn't show it. I am worried*

that when I do get married and have kids they won't have a granny from my side of the family.'

---

'My real parents split up when I was only 3. I was very young and didn't understand. Now I live with an aunt and uncle. My aunt is my father's sister. Not long ago they started fighting really badly and I was afraid they were going to split too. I hate them for what they did to me by bringing me up hating my mum. I don't think people should be allowed to get married until they're sure it's going to work. There should be a probation period so if things don't work out there is no harm done.'

---

'My parents have already separated. It was hard at first, but I realize that my parents are probably much happier now.'

---

'About three years ago my parents came very close to separating. The thing that is worst is the violence of it all. There seemed to be such hatred between the two of them. My sisters and I didn't seem to be considered at all. The most horrible thing was going to bed and trying to hide under the quilt and singing to myself so that I couldn't hear all the shouting. All that I wanted to do was to ignore it all and pretend that it wasn't happening. It makes you wonder why they got married in the first place – they seem to have no common interests at all. The problem seems to be a total lack of communication and now this has rubbed off on me and I find it very difficult to talk openly and honestly to people.'

---

'My parents have separated, but they are not divorced yet. It doesn't feel that bad, but it's not like I'm glad he's gone. It's quite the opposite. I see him fairly often but he has just moved quite far away because of work. I can't say I miss him because I still see him. After he had gone I found it hard to tell my friends, even though most of my friends' parents are divorced. I think all my friends know now, but most didn't find out from me. Some did – but only the ones I wanted to know.'

------------------------------------------------

'I am now fostered after my parents divorced seven years ago. At a younger age, I was very selfish in my views on whose fault it actually was, and 'why did it have to happen to me?' But realizing that I wasn't the only one in this world whose parents have separated, I got on with my life, treating it like a 'fact of life'. It was neither of my parents' fault. In my mind it was just one of those common factors that neither could live with the other any more. Not meaning that they hate each other but just that they had difficulty putting up with one another. Of course I still cry and wish it hadn't happened, but it's now too late to turn the clock back. As far as I am concerned, you just have to get on with life, otherwise you don't get anywhere and become one big drop-out!'

------------------------------------------------

'I used to wonder whether I was adopted or something, that maybe Mum and Dad were not my real mum and dad and they had never told me. It's not that I'd mind being adopted. It's just that I'd like to KNOW. I worry about everything, and get myself so worked up I can't sleep. I lie awake until the problem is solved in my mind.

**6th March** Drama of the week – Daisy was caught shoplifting at the local Tesco's. Only a very large bar of chocolate. She and Aunty Jo were marched off to the manager, and threatened with the police, but Mum pleaded Daisy needed medical help, not prison help. I blame Uncle Geoff. Daisy's been crying ever since, saying it was all an accident. Managed to make her laugh with a joke: 'What's the difference between brussel sprouts and bogies?' Answer: 'You can't get kids to eat brussel sprouts!'

Can't take much more. Thank goodness this German invasion is nearly over. Aunty Jo's been found a temporary army house outside London, until things are sorted out. Just when I've become Paul's heroine. At least one boy likes me, even if it's a bed-wetting 8-year-old. It's because I encouraged him to send off a green crisp he found in a packet of Salt and Vinegar, with an 'it's not good enough' letter. Five packets came back by return of post – one given adoringly to me.

School meeting about Paris trip today – sounds great.

# 6 **Drunken** French **Louses**

**14th March** Just got my diary back. There are some nice people around in the world. I was sure someone had stolen it and accused everyone in sight, Pete, Mum and Daisy being the prime suspects because they're all so nosy. Don't think they realized how unhappy it made me – not having it to write in.

I hate losing things. Couldn't think of anything else at first. Was really angry, but then I began to forget about it and decided not to keep another diary. Today a parcel arrived through the post for me. Couldn't understand it as it wasn't my birthday or anything. Don't know where it came from – no note or anything, just my diary. Hope someone had a good read – as long as they don't know me!

Pete's been on at me to write the 'sex and contraception' article for the school mag.

**15th March** Paris tomorrow – cool idea. Got to be up by 5.30 a.m. and at school by 6. Dad says he'll take me. My room's a complete tip. Don't think anything I've got suits me. Mum's furious and says I can't go till my room's tidy. No sympathy for the fact that I'll look a complete Sharon.

Pete's promised to look after Pinko while I'm away. Promised not to experiment on him, but said not to blame him if he died whilst I was away – because it would be from MSS (missing Susie syndrome).

**16th March** Via Tunnel sur le bus. Didn't see any refugees walking the other way. Kate, Emma, John, Winston and I all sat on the back seat and shared our lunch. Wished Sheila had sat at the front, as she was threatening to throw up all the time. When we got to France, we waved at all the Frenchmen in the cars behind. Good response! Different from back home. Wish Sita had been able to come too, but her parents wouldn't let her. Don't know why not – just overprotective, I guess.

We stopped off for coffee on our way through Paris. Saw the Eiffel Tower and went down the Champs-Elysées past the Arc de Triomphe. Then over the Seine, which is full of crap but at least there were all these beautiful barges with gardens on them, and children scootering around their decks. Wish I could live on one of them and do the same.

It's going to be a really good holiday. Coffee, cakes and wine all the time. Mr Rogers, our form teacher (who used to teach Pete 'the facts of life' and has been in the school for ever), is in charge. He refers to me as 'clever Pete Payne's little sister' – he's a creep but a nice one. He always runs the French trips. I think he's having an affair with the French mistress, Miss Dunlop, who always comes too.

**19th March** 🗼 Chere Diary – je suis très fed up with this exchange business. J'arrived here three days ago and je ne peux comprend pas un word of what anyone is saying to me. Totally fatiguée by the end of the day trying to understand and to parler la langue. Madame Cerveau is very gentille to me. Much better cook than Mum but she doesn't understand about moi not eating meat. She couldn't have understood my letter and I can't explain now. Madame looked très upset when I left her best roast veal, but I'm not going to eat any poor little calf that's been shut up in a wooden box all its life, and I'm definitely going to count snails and frogs' legs as meat! Had to give in over fish or they'd have been convinced I was mad – but I won't tell Pete.

I share a room with Marie – but she goes off and sees her friends without me tout la temps. I know Madame tells her to stay with me – but she jamais does. Last night Madame allowed us to go out to un club and Marie abandoned me. NO ONE asked MOI to dance except a real grease-gun midget with spots the size of saucers.

Luckily Madame had insisted on us being back by 10 o'clock – she's very strict – so the agony was short.

They all laughed and said I was a 'tapisserie' – I found out that meant 'wallflower'. I think I'm going to pleut.

**20th March** 🗼 Now I know why I'm so miserable – I'm on the blob again, a week early and I've forgotten to bring ma Tampax. Mum had warned me my period times might get upset by travelling. I've got terrible cramps and haven't even got the Mefenanic acid tablets the doctor gave me to use when they get bad. I'd been having time off school each month before I got them. Perhaps that explains my maths report! These tablets have made all the difference to the agonies – much better than aspirin and the other things I've tried.

Went for a 'promenade' to suss out a magasin that might sell Tampax. Didn't like to ask Madame or Marie. How could I? Only just arrived and immédiatement I'm asking for la Tampax. Madame doesn't like me wandering around on my own. Wanted to send Marie's younger brother with me. No way.

At the local supermarche they were right up on the top shelf. Had to ask twice in my best French, 'Avez-vous de Tampax si vous plait?' Whole place – packed with old men – went silent. The shop assistant climbed up, muttering 'De Tampax, de Tampax, toujours de Tampax', pulled out the bottom one, and they all fell on his head, along with a load of serviettes sanitaire. Quelle horreur! Très, très embarrassing.

**23rd March** Madame took Marie and me to Paris yesterday by train. Loved the metro, loved the Quai d'Orsay, loved the open-air markets, loved the Tuilleries, where we sat eating baguette sandwiches and drinking coke (along with the other 200,000,000 daily coke drinkers around the world). Madame bought us une crêpe au chocolat for dessert. We passed a magasin called 'Preservatifs': a whole shop devoted to condoms – every colour, flavour, shape and size. Pretended not to look while actually feasting. Madame and Marie showed no embarrassment. Je pense que les Françaises sont tres liberal. Used a pissoir outside the Pompidou Centre which played music while I peed. Five euros for a pee seems un peu cher. Un très exhausting day.

**26th March** A letter from Pete! First one he's ever written to me. Not much of a letter though. Think Mum made him do it. All it was was a scribbled note on the front of a 'Message to Young People'. It said 'Susie – I'm very worried about you, in France with all that wine, so I'm sending this leaflet to make sure you're not getting totally pissed all the time.

Hope you find it useful! Your loving and concerned brother – Pete'.

Personally, I would have liked him to have kept the leaflet for himself and sent me some juicy news about things like 'How he and Brenda are getting on', 'Has Bovril had her kittens yet?', 'What Sam's up to', and 'Have Daisy and Paul gone yet?'.

## How to tell when drinking is becoming a problem

- Do you drink because you have problems and have to face up to stressful situations?
- Do you drink when you get mad at other people, your friends or parents?
- Do you often prefer to drink alone, rather than with others?
- Are you starting to get low marks? Are you skiving off work?
- Do you avoid being honest with others about your drinking?
- Do you ever get into trouble when you are drinking?
- Do you often get drunk when you drink, even when you do not mean to?
- Do you think you're big to be able to hold your drink?

## Alcohol Consumption in Different Countries

| Country | Consumption of litres of pure (100%) alcohol equivalent per year per person |
|---------|-----------------------------------------------------------------------------|
| France | 12.7 |
| Spain | 10.8 |
| Portugal | 9.8 |
| Italy | 8.7 |
| Australia | 8.4 |
| UK | 7.6 |
| USA | 7.5 |
| Japan | 6.5 |

**28th March** 🅰 There's lots of time, but doesn't seem to be any privacy for writing this diary. Even the toilets in other people's houses aren't the same sanctuary as at home.

**29th March** 🅰 Un visite to EuroDisney par autobus avec mes amis – following the Mickey Mouse signs. When we arrived we joined the conveyor belt of wide-eyed kids and got transported to a squeaky-clean fantasy land.

For little kids, I dare say the place was great. They could feel like Cinderella, explore a jungle, become a spaceman, all within a couple of hours. However, at our great age, I think although part of us wanted to believe, the other part was more than a bit cynical!

On the 'high street', we met a lady holding a bunch of balloons with a smile that was really sinister. She had spent two months in this 'Wild West' land and had not been outside the place. She whispered that she was constantly being watched by 'foxes' and she couldn't wait to get back to Birmingham where she lived. The 'foxes', she insisted, were undercover employees who kept an eagle eye on the staff to ensure their endearing smiles were maintained. Just our luck, we thought, meeting a paranoiac straight off. But then we came across 'Tigger' in the main square, who started to dance around with me, flirting and waving his willy-like tail. This was considered too frisky even for 'Tigger', and he was carted off by a couple of French gendarme characters with the order to 'get the hell back to the Alice in Wonderland tea party'.

Our behaviour overstepped the mark again at the car race track. John was a bit over the top in aggressive driving and was hauled out of his car for driving too fast and crossing the finishing line 'before your turn'. Had a bit of a feeling that 'big brother' Mickey was always watching from behind his plastic head.

**30th March** On our way home. Relief to be back with my friends again and to speak English for a change. Kate's French family was upset she ate so little. John's family were all alcoholics. He was surprised they didn't have wine coming out of the taps, they drank so much. Mr Rogers was sitting on the seat in front, overhearing us. Breathing out heavily alcoholic and smoke-laden breath, he added that it wasn't just the French who had problems. In 2000 in the UK, the government spent £29,500,000,000 of our money on the National Health Service, and the same amount on education. And as individuals, we spent £10,000,000,000 on tobacco, £24,500,000,000 on alcohol, and £45,000,000,000 on food.

The government are total hypocrites, collecting £200 a second from alcohol taxes and only spending 0.1 pence per second on advertising its dangers. Really depressing. He said that alcohol drinking was involved in half of all murders, one in five of all child abuse cases, over half of all suicides, and a quarter of road traffic accidents where somebody is killed. I'm sure he knows the facts. He informed us that we didn't need to become alcoholics. With alcohol-free wines, beers and ciders, we can still look 'hard' and drink at the same time.

Sheila laughed at my Tampax problems. She'd brought hers with her. She'd tried throwing her used ones into the lav, but they wouldn't flush away. She had to fish them out again, smuggle them through the house in a drippy paper bag, and throw them into the dustbin.

Saw an advert for using condoms as we were leaving Dover: 'Taking a condom on holiday with you won't save your life, using one might.' John said it was a bit late, seeing we were on our way home, and why were condoms called 'French letters' anyway? Mr Rogers didn't know that, but said there was a legend that the sheath was invented by a Dr Condom, who was doctor to King Charles II. A real fount of knowledge – he also knew (and I wonder how?) that randy Italians in the 16th century were using linen sheaths to stop themselves from getting syphilis. Quite funny really, seeing that everybody is now starting to use sheaths again to avoid getting all the nasty sexually transmitted diseases around, including chlamydia. Anyhow, Mr Rogers said that if they bothered to teach Latin in schools nowadays, we'd know that the word 'condom' actually comes from the Latin word 'condus' meaning 'a receptacle'.

There was a funny smell when we were unpacking the cases from the bus. One of the bottles of wine John was bringing back for his next party had broken. He couldn't believe that wine was still so cheap in France compared with England. Think he's become addicted while living with his French family.

**1st April** Slept all day yesterday – exhausted after journey back and by playing with Bov's kittens. Glad to say Pinko is alive and well, so Pete's kept his word, though I do need to sort that bighead out.

Got up knowing it was April Fools' Day but was fooled all the same. On way to newsagents greedy me saw a pound coin on the pavement outside John's house. Tried picking it up – burst of laughter from behind a hedge. He'd stuck it down with Super Glue. Total failure at catching Pete out. Even tried 'Brenda's on the phone' to get him out of bed, and he's much too clever for the salt in the sugar trick. Did catch Dad with my monster box of chocolates marked 'SUSIE'S CHOCOLATES – DO NOT TOUCH'. A great springing monster bonked him on the nose when he tried stealing one. Think he was more annoyed at getting caught out than anything else.

Pinko's got anorexia. Either that or she's been starved. Actually Pete appears to have done nothing! The cage was filthy, and if she did get anything to eat, it was because Mum stuffed an occasional cabbage leaf in. But me – I seem to have put on weight when I was in France. I was 62 kilos this morning – help, help.

Am back to being an unembarrassed vegetarian. Mum knows my ways, and it's good not to have to eat 'veggies without the meat' all the time. It's not that I'm totally committed – like vegans, who don't even eat milk or eggs or cheese or anything. Vegetarianism makes real sense to me. You can get all you need to survive if you make sure you have all the proteins and vitamins – and Mum's outstanding on reading the labels. Pete thinks it's mad to eat lentils, cheese and beans to get protein when you can have 'a fat juicy steak' instead, but at least I won't get BSE.

**4th April** At last, with all her huge experience – ha ha. Louise has started to write her 'guide to boys'…

---

### My Guide To Boys
#### by Louise Heathers

*BOYS…BOYS…BOYS…BOYS…BOYS…BOYS*

*– or why I hate them. When I most want them to notice me, they don't. I spend hours getting done up and they don't even notice. I suppose it might bring a bit of excitement into some girls' lives, but I just find it obnoxious. When I'm insulted and sulk and I'm waiting for them to apologize, they don't, cos they think it's not macho to say sorry.*

*Occasionally I have these fantasies about the boy of my dreams arriving on my doorstep with a huge bunch of flowers, ready to whisk me away on a huge red motorbike. Some chance!!!*

*I try to pretend not to be the slightest bit interested. This actually is an awful lot harder than it sounds. When someone I fancy saunters over to borrow my homework, how am I supposed to say 'No' in a calm and collected voice, when my stomach is raving and my knees are jelly? Then all I get for my pains is that they go off with my best friend. Boys like that just aren't worth the bother.*

---

This certainly isn't the way I feel about boys. She's even more desperate than I am.

**6th April** No boy with a nose would come within a mile of me at the moment, as I stink of anti-louse stuff. Paul's leaving present to the family when he, Daisy and Aunty Jo finally left was nits. Aunty Jo admitted it to Mum in one of their endless phone calls. I had thought it was just dandruff when I felt itchy in France. Hope my nits enjoyed their French holiday. Mum found the little beasties when she examined my hair.

Dad – the beastie exterminator – was in his element. He said that in a recent survey asking mums whether their children had had head lice in the previous year, one in three said 'Yes'. But worse was to come. If our heads were looked at by a 'beastie hunting' expert, they were FIVE times more likely to find them than our mums. On average, the beasties have been feeding away on our heads for four months before we know we've got them.

Dad was even willing to give us the facts about the louse's sex life. The life of a louse is a mere 3 weeks. They like everybody's hair but some more than others. They prefer short hair to long, clean hair to dirty (no, that's not a mistake). They seem to spread only directly by head-to-head contact, they cannot jump, hop, fly or swim, and they can spend time on several heads a day.

What the head louse does when it gets onto your head – between the hairs – is to take a good bite at your skin (up to 200 bites a day per louse). When it bites, its spit irritates your skin and makes you want to scratch. Having bitten and sucked out a little bit of your blood, it then shits. When you scratch, you rub their shit into the bites and the irritation gets worse. The next thing they do (at 7 days of age) is start having sex (which I haven't managed yet, though I wonder whether Kate has) and laying eggs, which they attach to the roots of your hair. A short but not such a lousy life after all.

To stop this grossness you first have to find the beast, which is the hard part. Mum needed her glasses to find them, as they are nearly transparent and a bit smaller than the head of a match, and the eggs on the hair are pinhead-sized and flesh-coloured. Dad was really mean and cruel. He said that regular combing breaks the legs off the lice. Life is not so easy for a legless louse and they fall off our heads and die. (If animals can feel pain, then why can't lice? What about Lice Rights?)

Mum made the whole family use the smelly anti-louse lotion. Luckily – if used properly – it not only kills the lice but protects you for a bit against getting them again. We had to leave it on overnight and couldn't go swimming for 2 days after we'd used it or blow-dry our hair (chlorine in water and heat stop it working).

EASTER HOLIDAYS begin today – so don't have to stink out the school.

**7th April** Going to have a spending spree. Blow all my saved money. Messaged Mary to come too. She rang back and said that she'd love to – amazed she's actually leaving her boff's side to grace me with her presence.

**8th April** Caught up on some gossip with Mary yesterday and had a laugh trying on outrageous outfits in Miss Selfridge's. So annoying – unless you're thin and leggy, none of the clothes fit or look good. Mary thinks it's stupid to diet and we're all right as we are. She may be – but I feel less certain for myself.

Still, why should we try to be like the models in the adverts? They're all touched up and specially photographed to look thinner than they really are, anyway.

I think all those French painters we saw had it right – no clothes and none of that 'oh so thin' rubbish. Pete says that boys don't really like thin girls, and that it's their minds and personalities which matter. Don't believe a word of it. Mary saw him at the cinema without his glasses and with his hand down the top of 'all-breasts' Brenda's blouse. She says the air was heavy with testosterone. I suggested to Pete that his mind was on Brenda's body, especially as she doesn't have any personality. He shouted at me to mind my own f…..g business. Don't know where he learns this kind of language.

# Glands, **Fevers** and
## Not Having **Babies**

**10th April** Feel awful – hate myself – especially the bit called my throat, which is so sore. My tonsils feel like two mountains with someone gouging them with blunt knives. If I survive, I promise never to think those thoughts about Sam again.

No sympathy from Mum. She's never believed any of us when we say that we're ill since she found Sally out shopping half an hour after she'd claimed she was at death's door. Pete just did his 'I am the world's number 1 budding doctor' act – told me to shut up and take a paracetamol. Bloody know-all.

What a waste of holiday.

**11th April** Worse – Sam, Sam, where are you? Actually anyone who would be nice to me would do.

**12th April** Worse, worser, worstest. Pete still doesn't believe I am really ill. 'How can you be going on about your sore throat when half the Third

World is starving and the other half is dying from malaria and TB' was his response. He won't come close to me though. Don't want him to, but wish Sam would.

**13th April** Worstest of all. It's supposed to be Good Friday – nothing good about it and it's Friday the 13th. Mum talked to the doctor, who said most sore throats are due to viruses or bacteria, but you usually can't tell which, so just to give paracetamol or aspirin. Big deal. Aspirin for this, aspirin for that. Nowadays, it's even aspirin for heart attacks. Thousands of years of medical science and that's all they come up with?

Sam called to see Pete today – didn't even come up to see me. I hate him, I hate Pete, I hate the world. I'm going to stay in bed and starve for ever and ever, and then they'll all be sorry.

**14th April** Dragged down to the doctor's by Mum. Much the illest person in the waiting room. The doctor was OK but made things worse by poking the back of my throat with a stick. Said she'd send it off to see what grows. Yugh – monsters with knives for claws probably.

She then sent me to see the nurse, who took all of my blood into a syringe – seemed there would be none left for me. I asked her if she had had a starring part in *Interview with the Vampire*. I turned pale and droopy at the end of the needle. Told Pete, and he said I was like that all the time.

**15th April** Dad did his usual Easter egg hunt. Strange, but I still enjoy these Easter rituals, raw tonsils or not. So does Pete, who stole all my eggs and ate them, saying I was too fat already, and with my sore throat, wouldn't want them anyhow. Tried to get my own back by saying I'd tell Mum about him and Brenda. She's someone Mum wouldn't approve of. He said 'go ahead, I only wish there was something to tell'.

Not much fun having Easter and feeling so awful.

**20th April** The nurse from the doctor's rang yesterday to say 'Susie has got glandular fever'. So I am ill, even if no one else believed me. Funny thing is, I don't feel so bad now – just floppy and exhausted, like a sopping wet rag.

Pete keeps making kissing noises at me since he read the 'Glandular Fever' leaflet the nurse gave Mum. (But I haven't kissed properly since Christmas. Then it was John, who smells awful and tried to touch my breasts.)

# Glandular Fever

### (1) WHAT CAUSES IT?

A virus called the Epstein Barr virus (after the men who first discovered it).

### (2) IS IT CATCHING?

Yes – it is an infectious disease and is spread from one person to another. However, it's not very infectious and usually you have to be in close contact with a person who has it in order to catch it. That's why it's sometimes called the 'kissing disease', but kissing isn't the only way of getting it. It can also be spread from one person to another like a cold – by breathing in the virus or swallowing it.

### (3) WHO GETS IT?

It is very common, and about one in 10 children aged 14 and 15 have had it, often without knowing. By the age of 18, over half of young people will have had it. Boys and girls get it about equally, and adults can get it too.

### (4) HOW DO YOU KNOW THAT YOU HAVE GOT IT?

You nearly always get a sore throat and swollen glands in your neck. If it's glandular fever, these do not get better as quickly as sore throats and swollen glands normally do. Other glands may also swell up in your groin or under your arms. Sometimes you even get a rash. You'll usually feel tired, unwell, and will have a headache and a fever.

### (5) HOW CAN YOU PROVE THAT YOU HAVE GOT IT?

You have to see your doctor, who can do a blood test. This will usually but not always show whether or not you have glandular fever (or whether you have had it in the past). There are also other viruses that can make you feel unwell in the same way.

## (6) HOW LONG WILL IT LAST?

This varies. Some young people get it and then get better so quickly that they do not even realize they have had it. For most, it lasts about three weeks.

First week – very sore throat, swollen glands, temperature; you will feel very unwell and want to stay in bed.

Second week – fever going down, and you will feel a bit better.

Third week – you will feel much better; fever has gone, but you will still feel very tired, even when doing very little.

## (7) CAN IT LAST FOR YEARS?

Normally you get better in a few weeks, but you may still get tired very easily for some further weeks, or months, afterwards. For a few people the effects last even longer.

## (8) IS THERE ANY TREATMENT?

None at the moment – though you may be given an antibiotic by your doctor when you first have a sore throat, before it is realized that you are suffering from glandular fever. This won't do you any harm, but neither will it help cure the glandular fever, because antibiotics don't kill viruses (only bacteria). The only treatment is to take paracetamol regularly (always check the instructions on the bottle or packet to see how much, and how often to take it). This will help bring your fever down, help relieve the pain in your throat, and will generally make you feel a bit better.

## (9) SHOULD YOU STAY IN BED AND REST A LOT?

Whether you stay in bed or not depends entirely on how you feel. For the first week or two most people do feel like staying in bed, or at least resting, sleeping, and having drinks and food that is easy to swallow – jellies, soups, ice-creams. Later on you may still feel like resting and sleeping more than usual. Your body, under these circumstances, is usually very good at telling you how much you can do.

## (10) WHAT ABOUT PLAYING SPORTS?

It is not a good idea to do sports in the first three weeks of the illness, and you probably won't feel like it. You may even get very tired after mild exercise for weeks or months, so be guided by how you feel.

## (11) WILL IT AFFECT YOUR WORK?

During the first weeks of the illness most people find it very difficult to work and concentrate. When you get back to school, it's best to tell your teachers what's been the matter and they should be sympathetic. Show them this leaflet if they aren't! Most children find work a problem for some weeks after the illness because of tiredness, depression and lethargy, but it does get better and everyone recovers.

## (12) IS GLANDULAR FEVER THE SAME AS CHRONIC FATIGUE SYNDROME?

No. Chronic fatigue syndrome is also known as ME, or myalgic encephalitis. Other names include 'Yuppie flu' and 'Post-viral syndrome'.

What people complain of with Chronic Fatigue Syndrome is: aching in the muscles after exercise, excessive tiredness, poor concentration, memory loss and depression. There has been a lot of discussion about whether this really exists as an actual disease. Nobody has managed to find out what causes it. We do know that a small number of people who have glandular fever, flu, or some other viral nasty can go on to get these sorts of problems, which may last for months.

There is no specific test you can do to tell whether or not you have chronic fatigue syndrome. It usually gets better by itself.

**24th April** Kate told me I'd missed a timed essay for GCSE English – will I fail? Made Mum give Pete a note for school. The teachers always think you're just skiving even if you're dying.

**2nd May** Mum spoke to my teacher. Hate her doing that but it seems I haven't missed out on my GCSE. My teacher said that if I had missed an essay, all they would do is take the best of the ones I have already done.

Horrible fright today – thought Bovril had broken her leg. She was limping around trying to keep up with her kittens. She's only just back from being 'done' at the vet's. I found this huge bump and something sticking out of it. I panicked and rang Mum at work. She came home at lunch-time and said it looked like a bee sting. Then I remembered that Bov had been playing around with a bee – trust her to pick the first bee of the year. We removed the sting very carefully and then Mum said to leave Bov alone.

She also said that if it had been me that had been stung by a bee, I should have put some bicarbonate of soda (mixed with water) on the swelling, and that if it had been a wasp, some vinegar. Said it is easy to remember which is which because it's 'Bee for bicarbonate and Winegar for wasp'.

Mum said that some people have a very bad reaction to a sting. They get massive swelling around it, which can spread. If this happens (it is quite rare), they need a doctor – quickly.

Dead bored being at home, dead tired if I try doing anything else. Searched Pete's room – found this book of jokes in his wardrobe (along with three old copies of *Playboy* and a couple of other girlie mags). Light relief at last, so cheered up. Here are some of the jokes…

* If it moves – fondle it.
  - *Don't take the piss out of beer – it needs all the flavour it can get.*
* Why is virginity like a balloon? – one prick and it's gone.
  - *100,000 lemmings can't be wrong.*
* Support the wild life – vote for an orgy.
  - *If at first you don't succeed – forget it.*
* If you've got fluid on the knee – you're not aiming straight.
  - *People who live in glasshouses should have sex in the basement.*
* Y-fronts prevent fall-out.
  - *I'm perfectly well adjusted – but you can fiddle with my knob.*
* Definition of a man – the redundant end of a penis.
  - *Keep Britain green – have sex with a frog.*
* Photographers do it in the dark.
  - *Teachers do it with class.*
* Keep pop music alive. Kill the producer of 'Top of the Pops'.
  - *What's brown and taps at the window? – a baby in a microwave.*
* Adam came first, men always do.
  - *Careful – after peeing, give it more than two shakes and it's wanking.*

Why are boys' minds always in their pants, I wonder? And Pete always seems to have girlie magazines around – why?

**6th May** Pete's nagging me about the article on sex and contraception. Thinks I've got nothing better to do, just because I'm ill. He's revising away for his A and AS levels. I should be revising for GCSE, but I can't concentrate. Pete gave me a pile of contraception leaflets, to copy out the best bits. Must be anonymous, though – can't have the whole school thinking I know anything about it because then they will assume that I've done it.

## You, Sex and Contraception

What I think is: first – you don't have to have sex.

This article, *Sexual Behaviours in the UK*, says that 75% of girls and 70% of boys aged 16 haven't had sexual intercourse yet (OK, they have done some of the other things together!), so you don't actually have to have intercourse to be part of the 'in' crowd.

Whether you have had sex or not, you need to know about sex and contraception.

*How good is your knowledge about contraception?*

*Test yourself on the following 16 easy questions.*

*(Answers on pages 65 to 67)*

1. Do you need to have intercourse to get pregnant?
2. Can the woman get pregnant if she doesn't have an orgasm?
3. Can you get pregnant if you don't both 'come' together?
4. Is withdrawal a safe method?
5. How long after making love does 'emergency' contraception work?

6. Can the first bit of 'cum' make the woman pregnant?
7. Can you rely on the 'safe period'?
8. During which days of her period is it 'safe' to make love without contraception?
9. What is the contraceptive injection?
10. Does the 'pill' help protect you against sexually transmitted diseases, including Aids?
11. Is it OK to use spermicides alone?
12. Are IUDs (coils) a good method of contraception for teenagers?
13. Do condoms help stop you from getting sexually transmitted diseases?
14. Can you only have sex by having intercourse?
15. Does the 'pill' make you fat?
16. How long do sperm survive in the vagina?

## Answers

1. ✖ No – if some of the man's sperm get near the entrance to the woman's vagina, they can swim up it, though this is very unlikely to happen!

2. ✔ Yes – female orgasm doesn't, as far as we know, influence whether a woman gets pregnant or not.

3. ✔ Yes – neither partner has to 'come' for pregnancy to occur, as the man can leak sperm before he ejaculates.

4. ✖ No – often the man doesn't pull out in time, and he may leak some sperm before he does. Remember that just one drop of semen contains enough sperm to populate the whole of New Zealand. Even so, it is better to pull out than not, if you are not using any other form of contraception.

5. It is effective if taken up to 72 hours (3 days) after making love (NOT after missing the last period). The sooner you take it, the better.

6. ✔ Yes – before a man ejaculates, he leaks a bit of semen, which may act as a lubricant but also contains sperm.

7. ✖ No – the 'safe period' is not a very reliable method. It needs to be taught and you need to be able to chart your periods, your temperature, and your vaginal mucus.

8. No day is 100% safe, but some are worse than others. If you have a regular 28-day cycle, then days 7 to 15 after the beginning of your period are the worst days.

9. The contraceptive injection, which you need to have only every 3 months, contains the hormone progesterone and is over 99% effective.

10. ✖ No – this is the method least likely to protect you against sexually transmitted diseases (even though it's a reliable way not to get pregnant – if you remember to take it, that is!).

11. ✖ No – it's not safe to use spermicides alone, but again, if they're the only thing you've got around, they're better than nothing and do help to protect against Aids.

12. ✖ No – they are not recommended unless you've already had a baby. IUDs can lead to an infection of your tubes and make you infertile.

13. ✔ Yes – this is absolutely true and is one of their huge advantages.

14. ✖ No – one of the best forms of contraception is all the lovely sexy things you can do and have orgasm without actually having intercourse itself.

15. Not taking the pill may make you fatter – if you get pregnant! A small percentage of women may get fatter on the pill, but you can almost always find one that suits you.

16. The average ones among the whole 300 million of them in each ejaculate survive for 4 days, but remember there is a lunatic fringe which may survive for 6 to 7 days. (The egg is more fragile. There is only one, and unless it becomes fertilized, it dies within 12 to 24 hours.)

## If you didn't score well on this

## you certainly shouldn't be scoring at all!

## Contraception

From what I've found out by reading, there's no ideal method of contraception. They've all got their pros and cons. What's certain is that you're very likely to get pregnant/get someone else pregnant if you decide to take a chance.

**How likely are you to get pregnant without contraception?**

❯ If you have sex when an egg has been released (about 14 days before a period), there's a 30% risk of getting pregnant. (This may not sound all that risky, but would you cross the road if there was a 1 in 3 chance of getting killed?)

❯ If you have sex somewhere around the middle of the cycle but not at the most risky time (when the egg is normally released), there is still a 20% risk of getting pregnant.

❯ At other times, the risk can still be as high as 10%. Most people don't know when they ovulate, and although the egg doesn't hang about waiting to get fertilized (it survives for just 12 to 24 hours), the sperm hang around for several days. So even if the egg isn't released until a few days after having unprotected sexual intercourse, there may still be some hungry sperm waiting.

## How do you choose which contraceptive

The important thing, if you are going to have sex, is to find out all about the different methods available, and then you and your boyfriend/girlfriend can decide which method is best for your relationship and go for it. You both need to feel 'happy' and safe with the method you are using. What's right for one couple is not necessarily right for another. If, after a while, you decide you don't like what you're using, you can always change your mind and try something different.

## What can happen...

She thought it was wrong to have sex before marriage. One night her parents were out and one thing led to another. He respected her views, but they both lost control. He meant to withdraw, **but he didn't**. He thought she should have been on the pill, **but she wasn't**. She thought he should have used a condom, **but he didn't**. She should have gone for emergency contraception, **but she didn't**. They should have talked about it, **but they couldn't**. She thought she was going to have a baby, **but she wasn't**. They shouldn't have been so lucky, **but they were**.

In one study, 70% of couples had had unprotected sex the first time they did it. You may get away with it once, but don't count on it.

## The choice

You can choose between condoms, the combined pill, condoms and the pill, the progesterone-only pill, the contraceptive injection, an IUD (coil), a diaphragm (cap), spermicides, the 'safe' period, the contraceptive sponge or withdrawal. It sounds like a lot of choice, but it's less than it seems, as many of the methods aren't very effective.

## Where to get it

You can go to your general practitioner, or any GP. Other places are family planning clinics, or a Brook Advisory (or other young person's) Clinic if there is one near you. Some schools run clinics in the lunch hour. The pill is free from your GP and from clinics. Condoms are free from clinics, and some GPs give them out free, or you can buy them at a chemist's or from machines in public toilets.

## Condoms

### How condoms work

A condom is a sheath of thin rubber which is rolled over the erect penis and stops the sperm getting into the womb.

### Why I like condoms

- ❯ 'They're easy to get hold of from chemists, garages, pubs'
- ❯ 'They protect me against sexually transmitted diseases'
- ❯ 'They help protect me against Aids'
- ❯ 'He has to pay for them'
- ❯ 'She has to pay for them'
- ❯ 'I don't have to take chemicals all the time'
- ❯ 'It's less messy afterwards'
- ❯ 'easy to carry around and make me feel that there might just be a chance!'
- ❯ 'They are very safe and well tested'
- ❯ 'I can get her to put it on me so that she knows we're safe'

### Why I don't like condoms

- ❯ 'It cuts down on the sensation'
- ❯ 'You can't trust a male to use one properly'

>> 'I worry all the time that it's going to slip off'

>> 'It's like making love with a ski glove on'

>> 'It's a passion-killer'

>> 'He'll think I'm cheap if I carry a condom'

>> 'It's like tying the knot and throwing it away makes me feel I'm getting rid of the whole population of America all at one time'

## Summary

Condoms are very effective – **98%** reliable.

You can buy them everywhere (well, almost everywhere).

They help protect you from sexually transmitted diseases, and they don't harm your body in any way.

## The Pill

### How it works

It contains two hormones – oestrogen and progesterone – which stop the woman's egg being released each month.

### Why I like the pill

☆ 'It's the safest method I know'

☆ 'I find it doesn't interfere when we want to make love, as we don't have to stop and fiddle around'

☆ '…really easy, I only have to remember to take the pill every day and it's done'

☆ 'After all, they're free from GPs or family planning clinics, and that's what makes the difference for me'

☆ 'makes my periods not so heavy and always on time, which I like, as it helps knowing when they're going to come'

⭐ '...don't have to worry, it's all her responsibility'

⭐ 'For me, I like being in control of my own body; after all, if something happens, it's me that gets pregnant'

⭐ 'It's so bloody convenient'

## Why I don't like the pill

⭐ 'It doesn't protect me against Aids, or other sexually transmitted diseases'

⭐ 'I keep forgetting to take it, and then I have to use condoms for a week anyway'

⭐ 'I don't like the idea of filling my body up with hormones'

⭐ 'My friend put on weight and had headaches when she was on the pill and I don't want that'

⭐ 'I don't think it's right her having to take those hormone things all the time. Must have some effects, mustn't it?'

⭐ '...I worry about the side-effects'

## Summary

**The pill is the best contraception** for not getting pregnant, as long as you remember to take it, but on its own it's not so good if you want to avoid Aids and other sexually transmitted diseases. One very good option, of course, is to use both the pill and a condom. There are some side-effects from the pill, but most women feel fine and don't have any problems.

**Minor side-effects** These might not sound minor to you, or feel minor when you're suffering from them, but most of them pass off or settle down if you change to a different pill.

- depression
- headaches

- going off sex (the most efficient contraceptive!)
- feeling sick
- tender breasts
- moodiness

Most women feel absolutely fine on the pill.

**The pill and cancer** There have been a lot of scares about this in the last few years. The pill will protect you from cancer of the ovary and cancer of the womb, which is good. But the pill does increase the risk of getting breast cancer (although this increased risk seems to disappear 10 years after stopping it) and cervical cancer.

**Smoking and the pill** These don't go together as you are more likely to get some of the serious side-effects of the pill if you smoke.

**The pill and blood clots** There is a slightly increased risk of blood clots with the pill, especially if you smoke and if you have a family history of heart disease or any type of blood clots. If so, be sure to tell your doctor as it might not be safe for you to be on the pill.

## The Progesterone Pill and Injection

### How it works

It contains one hormone – progesterone – which helps stop the woman's egg being released each month and thickens the mucus around the neck of the womb (cervix) to make it difficult for sperm to move through it and reach an egg. It also makes the lining of the womb thinner so it is less likely to accept a fertilized egg.

### Why I like the injection

# 'Once I've had it, I don't have to worry for three months'

# 'I really like the fact that I'm the one in control of my own body'

\# 'It made my periods much lighter'

\# 'I had the injection after an abortion and it was a real relief as I'd kept forgetting to take the pill'

## Why I don't like the injection

\# 'The doctor said it doesn't stop me catching chlamydia, Aids, or any other sexually transmitted disease'

\# 'After I had the jab, I got much fatter'

\# 'I don't like the idea of putting a hormone in which I can't get rid of for 3 months if it causes any problems'

\# 'When I had the injection, I kept on dribbling little bits of blood for 2 months, which was a real pain'

\# '...I worry about the side-effects'

## Summary

The contraceptive injection is over 99% effective, doesn't interfere with sex, but does not stop you catching a sexually transmitted disease, so if you go for it, use a condom as well. It can cause weight gain, irregular periods and bleeding, as well as headaches, tender breasts and acne. It may also make you moody.

## The Cap

### How it works

It is a piece of soft rubber which the woman puts into her vagina to cover her cervix (the entrance to her womb) and stop the sperm meeting the egg.

### Why I like the cap

⚡ 'I thought it would be really difficult, but it was just like putting in a tampon'

⚡ '…I like the cap better than the pill. I got fed up having to take the pill every day. I don't like the idea of taking hormones all the time. They might do something to my body'

⚡ 'The great thing about using it is you don't have to stop and fiddle about in the middle, like with a condom. I put it in before I know we're going to make love'

⚡ '… means I'm in charge'

### Why I don't like the cap

⚡ 'It all sounds really messy to me, and I don't like the idea of putting something inside me'

⚡ 'It's a real bother as it needs to be fitted by a doctor, so you can't just buy it over the counter'

⚡ '…not safe enough for me'

### Summary

The cap is a good method if you are really motivated and don't mind putting things in and out of yourself. It's **96% effective**, though young people seem to have a slightly higher failure rate – perhaps they don't always put it in, or check that it's in the right place, or use enough spermicide with it.

The cap gives you a bit of protection against sexually transmitted diseases, but **not as much as a condom**.

## Unreliable but widely used methods

### The 'natural' or 'rhythm' method

The idea behind this is to find out when you ovulate (the egg is released from the ovary about 14 days before the next period) by a combination of taking your temperature, noting changes in the vaginal mucus, and charting the dates of your periods. It's good in that you get to know the changes occurring in your body, and there are no side-effects (other than pregnancy!). But it's a very unreliable method unless you have regular periods, have been well taught, and are very careful – as sex needs to be limited to 'safe' days, rather than when you feel like it.

### 'Withdrawal'

This is when the man takes his penis out of the woman's vagina just before he ejaculates. The trouble is *it's not very effective*, as men often leak a bit of semen containing sperm before they ejaculate properly, or can't get it out in time! It also allows any sexually transmitted infections to get passed around. But if you're going to have sex, and there's nothing else, it's certainly better than nothing. But it's much, *much* safer to use one of the other methods.

## Emergency contraception

A lot of people don't know or do anything about emergency contraception. They just behave like ostriches, dig their head in, and hope it will be OK. In one recent study of women wanting abortions, 70% had known they were at risk of getting pregnant (no contraception or a split condom). If everyone at risk used emergency contraception, at least 100,000 abortions in the UK alone could be avoided.

There are two types of emergency contraception: pill or coil.

### Pill

These are sometimes called the 'morning after pill', but that term is totally wrong. In fact, you have *up to 3 days* (72 hours) in which to get hold of the pills. It's best to take them sooner rather than later – though there's no need to wake a doctor up in the middle of the night!

You can get the pills free from any doctor, young people's clinic, family planning clinic, or accident and emergency department of a hospital. You can buy them over the counter if you are 16 or over but will usually have to pay for them. If you know that you may have taken a chance, make sure you get emergency advice. It's much better than needing an abortion or having an unwanted pregnancy. The pills have very few side-effects and you can take them more than once without doing any damage, but it is not a method to use regularly – only in emergencies. And if emergencies are happening once a week, it's time you sorted yourself out, as you are only kidding yourself that you are not having sex.

It's very good at stopping you getting pregnant (98% effective), but it's no good at stopping you from getting sexually transmitted diseases. All you have to do is take two lots of pills 12 hours apart.

## Coil or IUD

Very few people know that if you have a coil put in up to 5 days after unprotected intercourse, it can work as emergency contraception and prevent you from getting pregnant.

It is probably best to opt for emergency contraceptive pills, but if it is more than 72 hours (3 days) after the event, and you've not done anything about it, go to a GP or family planning clinic as quickly as possible and get a coil put in. It can be taken out after your next period or left in if you want to continue with it as a form of contraception.

**So don't forget to get emergency contraception if you forget to use something in the first place.**

That's it – good luck!

**14th May** I was in a total state this morning – couldn't decide WHAT to wear. Went through three changes of clothing. As soon as I think I look slightly OK, I decide it's not good enough and I change again.

I'm back at school with GCSE exams in three weeks. Help – a massive catch-up needed. If I fail my exams, I'm not sure what I'll do. I'll probably blame myself for having been a lazy cow for the last 2 years – though it wasn't my fault I was ill.

I'll be a complete failure – a nothing. It's a terrible pressure, all these exams, especially as I don't know what I'd say to my friends if they asked me how I'd done and I'd failed. Mum says I can only do my best, but whatever she says I know she'll be sad if I don't do well. (Not even sure that Dad knows I'm taking the exams.)

I wish I could turn the clock back and begin my revision over. I've got Mrs Smith's revision plan to work to again. I'll really do what she says this time, unlike for mocks.

## REVISION PLAN

1) **Estimate the total number of working hours you have till the exams.** (I've got 14 weekdays with 3 hours to revise after school, plus 3 weekends with 5 hours for revising each day, which makes a total of 14 x 3 + 6 x 5, which = 72 hours.)

2) **Give equal time to each subject.** (I've got 8 to do, so that gives me exactly 9 hours revision for each.)

3) **At this stage, there is no way you can revise everything on every subject. Therefore decide – for each subject – what you know least about, and get that sorted first. If you have any time over, then, and only then, go over the stuff you know best.** (Told Mum that as I know nothing best, and don't have

time to revise everything, this is going to be tough. Nice Mum started asking me questions about history – all of which I could answer!)

4) **Only work for a maximum of an hour at a time and then have a break. After one hour your brain doesn't concentrate so well.** (Not sure whether my brain ever gets going – wish I was more like Pete.)

5) **Remember it's relatively easy to get half marks for each question. It is many, many times more difficult to get really high marks. It is therefore better to answer all the questions reasonably well than to answer half the questions really well.**

**18th May** I'm always late for everything. And I'm an optimist and think I can do much more than I actually can, but my revision is going well. There's no time to write my diary, but I'm feeling less tired, thank goodness.

Mum's in a state about Brenda. She thinks she's a bad influence on Pete. She smokes and goes to pubs, and Mum's sure she does drugs. (I know she does, and Pete knows it too!)

Bov's in a state about her kittens being given away. It's better than drowning them, but she doesn't understand that.

# Stopping Exam Panic, Unwanted Sex and Baby Fears

**4th June** Panic, panic, panic. I can't sleep, I can't stop eating, I can't concentrate. I'm tired all the time, I've forgotten everything I've ever learnt, I'm terrified of everything going blank when I see the exam paper. I can't do any revision as it all drains from my brain again.

Being at school's worse because of the mass hysteria – everybody is scared shitless! I think the staff are really pissed off. Mr MacIntosh – the head – did one of his 'Now then children, don't panic' speeches. Quite scary, with his wire specs, white hair and crinkled face. He looks about 7 feet tall up on stage. Went on about how…

*It may be too late to revise now. Most of you will experience panic at one time or another when faced with that dreaded moment when you are first given the examination paper. Some of the things that will happen when you read it are good. More adrenalin will be pumped round your body, your heart will beat faster, and you will become* generally more alert. However, some of your reactions may be less positive – being unable to concentrate, thinking your mind has gone blank, feeling sure that you know nothing.

So wouldn't it be good if there were a few very simple tricks to help you cope with the bad aspects of panic? Well, there are. They are things that have been learnt by people who have taken many, many examinations. They can help a great deal, but they need a bit of practising.

What really STOPS THE PANIC is if, instead of rushing in and being convinced you will never finish the exam paper in time, you spend a few minutes getting yourself organized before you start writing. Many marks can be gained as a result of those few minutes planning. So:

**First** – and foremost if you feel yourself panicking when you get the exam paper – count slowly to 10 before reading it. This will only take 10 seconds but will allow your nerves just that tiny bit of time to calm down.

**Second** – read the instructions carefully as to HOW MANY questions you have to answer. (You will not get one single extra mark for answering more questions than you need to.)

**Third** – read the instructions again and find out how much time you have for the examination as a whole. Then divide the number of questions you have to answer into the total time, and work out how long you can spend on each question. (5 questions in the 86 minutes left in a 90-minute exam – after the 4 minutes that it has taken you to do the things listed here – means about 17 minutes for each answer.) Spend ONLY that amount of time on each answer.

**Fourth** – read each question carefully, decide which ones you want to answer, and quickly write down notes on everything you know about each one BEFORE you start to write the full answer on the one you know best. The reasons for this are very simple:

    a) If each question is marked out of the SAME amount – say 20 – to get 12 out of 20 is fairly straightforward; to get 14 out of 20 you *have to be very good; to get 17 or more out of 20 you would have to know the topic inside out.*

*b) If you spend half the total exam time answering the question you know best really well, and then only manage two more answers of the five you should have done, then you might get 41 marks (17 for your excellent one and 12 for each of the others). But if you do all five just fairly well (12 marks each), you will get 60 – simple really.*

*Writing short notes at the beginning – on every question you are going to answer while your mind is still fresh – prevents you from panicking about not having anything to say on the ones you know least about.*

He ended by wishing us 'All the very best of luck' – nice but a bit pompous and it was easy for him to say all that, as he wasn't actually taking the exams himself – it was us that had the agony.

Pete's into A levels and AS levels. We're not allowed to talk about his exams. We get screamed at if we ask how they went. Don't know what he's making such a fuss about – he's such a boff, he's bound to do well.

Dad and Mum totally fed up today. They're thinking of going to live somewhere else till all the exams are over.

**5th June** Exams start tomorrow. Resolutions:

I won't panic

I will read the questions

I will look and see how much time I have

I will see how many questions I have to answer

I will write short notes first

I will do my best handwriting

I will have all my pens and pencils and my calculator with me

# HELP!

PS I must remember to take my hayfever spray regularly.

**6th June** The English exam was easy but I messed it up all the same. Didn't see the question on the last page. So much for my resolutions. I had tummy pains all the way through. Curse periods. I think examiners should make allowances.

It really made a difference – Mum and Dad being so relaxed with me about the exams – even if they couldn't stand all the tension around the house. Kate's mum hassles her every time she wants to go out. Even on a Friday night she gets at her – 'but what about your homework? Have you thought about the revision you need to do for the exams?' Right in front of her friends. It's really not on – would make me want to do just the opposite.

What do parents think? That we want to fail our exams? At least Mum and Dad seem to trust me (most of the time anyway). They remind me to have rests from work, and they bring me cups of coffee. Mum makes a special effort to have meals on time and to give me treats, but today Dad's hardly speaking to me. He spent half the evening picking the phone up downstairs and finding I was still talking to Kate. All we were doing was complaining to one another about how immature and weedy all the boys in our year are – there's not one that's the slightest bit fanciable.

**8th June** Maths OK. But Sheila wasn't. She walked out sobbing — half-way through. Everybody looked at her as she went. Nobody could understand. She's the brain of our class.

**9th June** Thank God for weekends. Kept to my revision timetable. One hour biology, cup of tea, one hour history, cup of coffee and a walk. All was well till I looked at an old GCSE history paper and couldn't answer two of the five questions. I'll never manage.

Messaged Kate and Emma to come for lunch. Kate messaged back that she couldn't make it for lunch, but came afterwards. I don't think she likes eating. It turns out the reason Sheila walked out yesterday was nothing to do with maths!

She'd been depressed for ages because a man had tried to rape her. It started last year when she got a job working part-time in a cafe belonging to a friend of her dad. It was OK for the first few months, but then the guy insisted on walking her home, even though she lived very near. During the Christmas holidays, every time he walked her home he tried to make her hold his hand but she didn't like it. She started to dread going there, but didn't want to give it up because she needed the money.

One night towards the end of January he was walking her home and holding her hand. Then, still holding her hand, he put her hand in his pocket. She suddenly realized that there was a hole in his pocket, because her hand was touching something warm and hard. She tried pulling her hand away. They were still walking towards her house and she couldn't say anything. When they finally got there, he let go and she ran in crying.

She felt she couldn't tell her mum, who wanted to know what was wrong. Sheila said that she was just tired, and went up to bed and cried herself to sleep. She didn't think she would hear from him again, but the next week, while she was out, he phoned and her mum said she could work that night.

Sheila felt incredibly scared and she was right. On the way home, although she'd told him she didn't want him anywhere near her, he tried to grab her and push her down an alley, in spite of the fact that there were other people around. Sheila said he was foul and smelt disgusting, but what was most scary was how strong he was. However, Sheila kept her head and her cool, perhaps because she had been expecting this to happen, and screamed very loudly. The guy swore at her and pushed off.

Sheila couldn't tell anyone, because she felt partly responsible, but she thought about it all the time. She hated that man and wanted to kill him. Since then she has stopped working, but she goes through it again and again in her mind, thinking about what she should have done. It made her feel so ashamed and humiliated. Once, when it all got particularly bad, she couldn't even kiss her father. She knew that if she did she'd be sick. Sometimes she blamed her mother and her best friend for not noticing that she was unhappy. She'd hinted but they'd never caught on. The exams were the last straw – but at least now her parents know.

Luckily I was able to tell my mum about the flasher who pulled out his shrivelled willy in the cathedral when we were on holiday in France. Eddie and Pete thought it was funny – but it wasn't for me. Mum's great. She said nothing happens in life that is so bad that you can't tell someone about it.

**11th June** History today – managed all five questions – hurrah! All that revision was worthwhile. French in the afternoon – un complet disastre, et je suis miserable maintenant.

Pete thinks that men like Sheila's boss should have their balls cut off. Mum says you can't do that, they need some kind of help. Still the same message from her. Everyone (including Pete) should know when to say NO – like my friend Jane did when we were 13 and it happened to her.

The only time it nearly happened to me was when some girlfriends and I were coming home across the park after a party. Some older boys followed us home, calling us 'slags' and making racist remarks about Sita. I don't know how Sita copes when people call her a Paki black bastard. I've never been so scared or I would have had a real go at them, but I thought they were going to rape us, especially as another girl, who was a bit drunk, was leading them on. Luckily, they went away after about 15 minutes. Since then I've tried to follow Sal's tips on being careful:

- ❯ if possible, stick to well-lit and well-used routes when going to and from school and people's houses

- ❯ always try to walk with someone you know

- ❯ never hitch-hike

- ❯ never play in or hang around in lifts or toilets

- ❯ only carry the money you need and don't advertise it in public

- ❯ try to tell your mum and dad where you're going and what time you'll be home

- ❯ if you go to a party, make sure you know beforehand how you're getting home

- ❯ if anyone tries to touch you in a way you don't like, say NO loudly and firmly, and tell someone about it

- ❯ if attacked, scream and run to where there are other people (better to run than to face the attacker)

- ❯ if you can't run, scream and kick, or knee the attacker in the balls, squeeze his windpipe, and try and gouge his eyes

I sometimes wonder why men *don't* try it on with me. Maybe I'm too ugly or too flat-chested. Pete says I don't need my self-defence lessons as I scare men off naturally. Maybe if I wait long enough, someone will come along who will love me for my mind, but I wouldn't mind being loved for my body a bit too.

**14th June** Revision programme has gone to pieces. Fed up with taking exams. Wish they were all over. Thank goodness my hayfever hasn't been so bad this year. Maybe the sprays have helped, or maybe there's been no pollen.

**19th June** The big day! THEY'RE OVER and there's a party at Mark's house. Mary came round to get ready at 3 p.m. The party wasn't due to start till 8. She looked great in her outfit. I was really jealous and had serious doubts about my new skirt, but Mary said it looked great. She's a good friend to have sometimes.

I tried some new lipstick – sort of dark rose colour – but it was too dark. I mixed it with some of the usual stuff and my lips ended up looking like a chocolate-covered raspberry. Talking about chocolate – I'm going on a 'no chocy' diet. I still weigh 62 kilos!

Got to Mark's just before 8.30. It was all Garage and R & B and I wished I'd worn my 501s. I felt a bit nervous as I couldn't see many of my mates, though some of Pete's were there, including Sam, so Mary and I went over. Mary was all over Sam like a bitch on heat and I felt insanely jealous. I stormed off to get myself a drink – hotly pursued by Sam, who gave me the 'What's up with you?' line. How could I possibly explain?

I picked up my drink and rushed off to the lav. When I came out, I came across Randy Joe and big-breasted Brenda heavily into business behind the settee. Not surprised Pete now thinks she's a slut. It's amazing she's not pregs yet, the way she goes at it.

I sat under the stairs for half an hour drowning my sorrows in drink. Don't know why I drink – it doesn't make me feel good, just depressed. While I was sitting there, someone I didn't know tried offering me an 'E' tab. No way was I going to try it. I think it's mental to use drugs. They should stay illegal to put people off using them. Though cigarettes and alcohol are drugs too – and I do use them. I think it is utterly wrong for people to make so much money from stuff that is killing people and destroying so many lives.

Boys are full of such shit with their corny 'chat up' lines. This guy continued, 'Here's 20 pence – go ring your mother and tell her you're not coming home tonight', and then 'Nice dress, think it would look good on my bedside table'. Told him to go get a life and that I wasn't so hot for boys with bum fluff on their faces.

Then Rahul came over to see if I was OK, and for some unknown reason (maybe the drink) I told him all about Sam. Rahul decided I needed cheering up, so he took me to meet a mate of his, Charlie – after I had checked the state of my mascara in the bog.

Charlie seemed a nice enough bloke, witty and not bad-looking – the sort of dark-haired, blue-eyed bloke you'd give your last Rolo to. We talked about music, school (he's leaving this term), and how boring the local area is getting. We actually had a lot in common (Toploader and Travis) and I felt really relaxed talking to him. He didn't put on a macho-bastard image when his friends came up, which was a change.

A bit later he asked me if I would like to take a walk outside, which made me a bit nervous. Some boys seem to see this as an opportunity to stick their tongues half-way down your throat, which can put a damper on the situation. I didn't want it to start getting heavy. But I felt no pressure from Charlie. He wrote down his telephone number and I gave him mine, but it will probably be a one-night stand – the kind of stuff dreams are made of. If he doesn't phone it was nice while it lasted, if he does I'll be over the moon.

**21st June** He hasn't rung. Stupid of me to think he would. Wonder if I should give him a ring to see if he's lost my number? I'd look a right fool if he hadn't and doesn't want to see me again. Why am I so sad?

Actually, I'm not sure that I do want to see him again. From something Pete said yesterday, I think he may be into the drug scene, and anyhow he's got dandruff.

**22nd June** Pact at school between Emma, Kate and me not to eat food that's bad for us. We're feeling lumpy after all that nervous eating over the exams.

Don't know what's got into Emma. She's stressed out at the moment.

**26th June** It's all a bit dodgy with Emma. We knew something was wrong but not how rough things are. She did it with Mark at the party – went the whole way, the lot. What a way to lose it – 'under the influence' at 2 in the morning when she couldn't get a lift home. And with that jerk Mark. She didn't let on till today, and now she's worried she's pregnant as she's a day late.

The whole thing was really mucky. Can't understand it – no condom, just spur of the moment stuff. Where's Emma been, for God's sake? She needs to grow up – but me saying all this is not going to help her now.

She knew a bit about emergency contraception from reading what I wrote but was too embarrassed to go to her doctor because it's the same one as her parents'. By the time she was really frightened, it was after the deadline. Now she's even talking 'abortion'.

**27th June** So far, I've managed not to eat:

chocolate for 2 days

cake for 4 days

sugar for 5 days

cream for a week

I did feel like a whale, but I'm certainly no minnow yet. Kate's lost 2 kilos – and she was only 45 kilos to start with. She says she wants to become a ballet dancer. If she's not careful, she'll become anorexic.

**30th June** Emma's still not come on. She borrowed a fiver off me yesterday to buy a 'pee' pregnancy test. Took the bus into town so as not to be seen in the local chemist. She hasn't rung me yet. She should know by now as they give instant results virtually immediately after a missed period.

Emma rang – so far so good, it was negative. Kate's persuaded her to go to the family planning clinic to have it double-checked.

# **Flab** is in the **Eye** of the **Beholder**

**2nd July** Message from Emma – 'prg tst ngtve – grt, grt, grt!' She's been given a load of condoms 'just in case'.

Dieting didn't last long. We've all stopped doing it except Kate. We decided it was stupid, but she's become obsessed. She wouldn't come to Coles for a celebratory 'end of dieting' tea. She made a feeble excuse about meeting her mother, but I'm sure it's her not wanting to eat. According to Mum, Sal went through a 'not-eating' stage for months, when she was doing her GCSEs, but it never got bad. Mum dug out a booklet she'd got for Sally at the time. Sal said the booklet was fine, but I could also look up all about it on the internet at www.doctorann.org because she had lots of stuff on it too.

# Anorexia

## Jenny's story

**66** I'm not sure how my anorexia started. All I do remember is wanting to be as thin as a friend of mine. I wasn't fat or anything. Just average size. But for some reason, I desperately wanted to be thinner, like my friend.

At this particular time – I must have been about 12 – I became aware that my brother was thinner than me, though I didn't really start dieting properly then. My mother had always been fussy about what my brother and I ate – mainly because of our teeth. We'd never been allowed biscuits or cakes, just the occasional sweet. You see my father was a big fat man, and my mother thought that there was nothing worse than having fat children as well.

It was in my second year at senior school that I decided it was about time I was the same size as my friend. I can't actually ever remember waking up wanting to diet. It was just a very gradual process.

A year later I was underweight and was diagnosed as severely anorexic. I was given a week to live if I didn't start eating.

I had gone through several changes in my eating habits. I started off having fruit for breakfast, pork pie for lunch, and a small dinner. I took ages to eat each item as I deliberately cut it into tiny pieces, the same way each day. My meals had to be at rigid times, and any later or earlier would be terrible. I can remember distinctly cutting up my pork pie into very small pieces and sucking each tiny particle of meat. Then my breakfast changed to a small piece of melon, and lunch to a scotch egg. (It had to be a very special one, and if I couldn't get it there was trouble.) I started doing lots of exercises too.

Life was hell for everyone and I cramped the whole family's style. Going out for a meal was a waste of time and money, and not just for me – no one enjoyed it. Then things got even worse, with no breakfast, a tiny salad with no chicken for lunch (my parents didn't know), and small pieces of cut-up vegetables for dinner.

My parents became very worried. It was now obvious that something was definitely wrong. (I suppose they had realized that for a long time but hadn't wanted to accept the situation.) My mother feared that I might have anorexia, and said that if I wasn't careful I'd have to be fed by a drip into one of my veins. I got angry with her and told her not to be stupid. How could a person as fat as me be told to eat and put on weight? The fact that I was many kilos less than all my friends never made it click that perhaps I was actually very thin. I continued my regular exercises and went on refusing to eat. I suppose you could say I'd become trapped in a vicious circle and my anorexia had completely taken me over.

However, on 12th November I had to go into hospital. (I was 14 at the time and 163 cm and weighed only 34 kilos.) But I didn't want any kind of help, though I do remember being made to have a small beefburger at McDonald's a few days before and thoroughly enjoying it. I hadn't had one for ages, and had forgotten how nice they tasted. However, there was no way that I was going to admit to liking it. My parents would have kept making me eat them and then I'd have felt guilty.

When I arrived at hospital I was told that if I didn't put on 9 kilos by Christmas I couldn't go home to spend Christmas with my family. Christmas meant a lot to me, and always had done, but my anorexia was so strong I didn't care whether I went home for Christmas or not. I just didn't want to put on weight. In the end I did go home – but for Christmas Day only.

In hospital I had to eat three big meals a day and three snacks with milky drinks containing a high-calorie powder. Eventually I reached my target weight and on 1st February was allowed home. I was relieved to be home again but my treatment continued, and I had regular family therapy meetings at the hospital as an outpatient.

When I had anorexia, there were lots of different reactions from everyone. My family were shocked and upset. It was difficult for them to understand my eating problems, especially my brother who loves his food. What a lot of people find difficult to understand is that anorexics absolutely love food. They love it so much that they're scared that if they start to eat they won't be able to stop. But their anorexics' powers are so strong that they won't let themselves eat and enjoy food.

My grandparents found it tormenting too. They had never heard of the illness. They said it had not existed in their day. They found it so weird that I should want not to eat all the time. Even now I don't think they fully understand.

The only person in my family who is anywhere near understanding is my mother. She has had a mild obsession with food so it is easier for her to help me than most other people. **"**

## WHAT'S ANOREXIA ALL ABOUT?

Anorexia nervosa occurs more commonly than you might think. It's not only girls who have the problem, but it is much more common in girls than boys. At least one in 100 teenage girls suffers from anorexia but only one in 2,000 boys. It usually starts in your mid-teens (it is much less common before the age of 13). Girls at boarding schools, fashion students, and ballet students are especially at risk.

There are lots of theories as to why it happens. For instance, it may be an expression of depression, a response to stress, an attempt to run away from the conflicts of growing up; it may be associated with a feeling of being totally hopeless at everything; or a fear of losing control over eating and becoming fat.

One common thread that runs through all these explanations is the stresses and strains being faced at this age by both sexes. The typical woman, for instance, is expected to be slim, beautiful, brainy, warm, loving, capable, kind, tough, business-like, etc. – ideals that a girl in her early teens may find rather frightening to live up to! To maintain control over at least one thing in her life – her weight – may therefore become an understandable obsession.

One thing all anorexics have in common is that they all overestimate in their minds how fat they are. Even though they may be thin and underweight, they think of themselves as fat.

## WHAT ARE THE FIRST THINGS THAT HAPPEN?

» you lose a lot of weight by deliberately not eating and/or exercising a great deal

» you get obsessed with the idea that you are fat and it's a dreadful thing to be

» if you are a girl, you stop getting your periods.

## WHAT OTHER THINGS CAN HAPPEN?

» your arms and legs become as thin as sticks

» your hands and feet become blue and very liable to chilblains

» you may not be able to sleep

» you may not be able to concentrate, though you may think you are being very clever

» you get very sensitive to cold

» your skin becomes dry and hairy over your neck, arms and legs

» your heartbeat rate slows down and down

» you may become increasingly sad and depressed

» you may become a compulsive user of laxatives (tablets which make you shit a lot and stop your food being absorbed, but which can also make you very ill).

## YOU SHOULD WORRY THAT SOMEONE IS BECOMING ANOREXIC IF THEY:

» become obsessed with food and cooking for others, but don't eat themselves

» get very thin

» seem restless when meals are being served, won't sit down to eat with other people, and mess about with their food instead of eating it

» leave the table before meals are ended (often to spit the food out somewhere or make themselves sick in the toilet)

» spend all their time weighing themselves and recording all the details

» do very devious things and behave very secretively

» tell everybody that they don't have any problems, especially with their weight

» take huge amounts of exercise, often overdoing things

» wear clothes which conceal that they are in fact very thin.

## IS THERE ANY TREATMENT?

At the moment we can't stop people from getting anorexia and there is a lot of argument over the best ways of treating it. However, most anorexics do get better, with only about one in three going back to having a problem, usually when they are under stress.

First, though, someone has to recognize that there is a problem, and this is usually not the person who has got it. Secondly, the person who has got it has to be persuaded that he or she does need help. It doesn't really matter who gives the help to begin with – parent, teacher, friend. After that, the family doctor is the best person to go to, who may then ask a specialist at the hospital for more help. Usually this can be given by regular visits to hospital, but if the anorexic is very, very thin, he or she might have to stay in hospital for several weeks. This is because anorexia can be VERY dangerous. Some people die from the effects of starvation.

## BULIMIA

Bulimia is another eating disorder like anorexia, and is sometimes part of it. At least two in every 100 girls have severe bulimia, and it most commonly starts around the age of 16.

Although lots of people go through periods of
chaotic eating, especially when they get stressed,
bulimia is worse than that. It often starts with
someone going on a strict diet, which is so
restrictive that they can't keep it up. They then
have an enormous binge – up to 30 times what they
normally eat – and then make themselves sick,
because they are guilty and frightened about
getting fat.

Often these binges are again followed by going
on a very strict diet. Sufferers yoyo backwards
and forwards between dieting and eating masses.
The best way of breaking into this cycle is to
stop intense dieting and to eat small regular
meals.

Mum says she read somewhere that if you put food on a very big plate, it makes the anorexic think that they are eating a smaller portion than they actually are. Myself, I can't understand how people can starve themselves.

Ate three jam tarts with cream and a whole Yorkie after reading all this.

**5th July** At last Pete seems to have found a proper girlfriend. It's Sandy (who used to go out with Randy Joe, whose been out with everyone, and is in the lower sixth). Kate says that her mum says that Sandy's dad is in hospital. I'm really pleased for Pete that he's found someone who likes him at last!

Think I may be addicted to shopping. Can't stop lying in bed in the morning and thinking about all the clothes I would like to buy…bras, knickers, jeans, tops, shoes, ear-rings, mmmmm. Must have a look at the internet and see what I can shop for there.

# Whose
## Job
### is it
## Anyway?

**6th July** It's strange not having to revise all day, every day. Don't know what to do with myself. Dad says that Pete and I should now be doing ALL the washing-up and housework. Mum let us off during the exams. Parents shouldn't have children in the first place if they can't cope with them.

I'm a bit scared of work experience next week. Sam's got a job with Pete unloading lorries at Debenham's. Wish I could work with him. That was my first choice. Second choice was trailing round with a barrister in the local courts. Would have really liked to do this too – fancied the murder, sex and violence. John got it instead. Maybe he'll tell me all the juicy details.

Actually I'm pretty angry. What have I ended up doing? Working as an assistant in a primary school, where nearly all the teachers are women. It's blatant sexism, though Mr Rogers said it just happened to work out that way. Laughable hypocrisy again. At least Emma's doing it with me.

98

**7th July** Raining, fed up, miserable, hopeless. Reminds me of what I went through when I was 13. At that age I used to think I was the only one with the miseries, but then I found out that a lot of others had them too. Sometimes I would come home from school, go up to my room and cry. I thought everyone and everything was against me, and I would have no life or friends – never ever. I thought my parents didn't care, that no one cared. I would talk to my teddy or Bov, as they couldn't answer back.

I remember Mum saying 'It's just your age'. If only I had known how right she was. I thought I was the only person in the universe who felt like that. I though that everybody else was blissfully happy, could do their schoolwork, and had friends they could talk to. At school we joke about it now and compare what we all went through – but I don't feel much like laughing and joking today. I tried watching video of *Bridget Jones's Diary*, but even that did nothing for me.

**8th July** Awful day. Mum said I couldn't go out unless I cleared up my room. I'm 16 and she treats me like a child.

**9th July** Better – first day at work experience. The children are really sweet but a bit much. Me and Emma couldn't step out into the playground for fear of being mobbed by a thousand 5-year-olds. One little girl jumped on me from behind, pulling off my MP3 heads and landing flat on her face on a step and cutting her lip. I didn't know what to do. There was blood everywhere. The lady on duty turned up and took her off to the secretary's office.

It's a real ego-booster to have 30 children looking up to you. Also, it makes me feel good knowing I can teach them something.

**10th July** Problems with the teacher I'm working for. She started off giving me one specific thing to do. Then when she saw how much I was enjoying piddling around helping in the drawing corner, she lumbered me with a great box of pencils to sharpen. Emma's having the same problems. We both had blisters to compare at the end of the day.

Also, the teacher gets angry if I get too friendly with the kids. Mind you, from the way some of them look I'm not sure I couldn't catch something from them. Classrooms are a prime breeding spot for nits, with the children working head to head and walking around with their hair touching. You can almost see the beasties crawling across. Having 'em once this year is enough for me, thanks. Told Dad about it when I got home. All he did was to get Mum to look at my hair to see if I had any living there – none at home luckily.

**11th July** Sent off by Mrs Joels to buy some labels for a project. The way some shopkeepers look at people my age is insulting. This one's eyes followed me everywhere. They think we're all shoplifting vandals. Wrinklies nick things too. Since when has being young meant you're a thief or generally something less intelligent than a piece of pasta? They're also always on about how we use bad language and are 'damn cheeky – not like in our day'.

Mum's getting on my nerves more and more too. I'll ask her a simple question needing a simple answer and she'll give me a long lecture – really gets me.

**13th July** Glad to be out of the clutches of those pestering little hands. Yesterday I just sat thinking 'don't touch me', but today I had to smile pleasantly while all my class kissed me goodbye and gave me cards. I enjoyed the variety of the work but think next time I'll make it clear from the start that no children will be allowed to hold on to me. At first I was so keen to fit in I didn't realize the consequences of letting them get close. Now I'm just relieved to be rid of all those demanding voices and the stupid teacher, who didn't even say goodbye or 'thank you'. I thought grown-ups were meant to set a good example.

Pete's perverse. Doesn't want me to go to parties which he's going to, even if I'm invited. Think Mum must have said something about Brenda. I told Pete it was paranoia on his part. He hates it when I use long words. He bet me I didn't know what it meant, but I told him, 'It's thinking people are getting at you when they're not'. I am a Health Freak too! He thinks he's the only know-all around, and says boys have bigger brains than girls. Told him yet again it's quality that counts.

Some people are leaving school this term – for jobs, training and unemployment. I'm furious because Sheila's dad won't let her stay on at school. He said that girls don't need to get an education as they are just going to raise a family. Neo-Victorian Fascist.

**16th July** Lovely letter from Rani, who's still having a good time in Birmingham though her parents don't know the half of it. I miss her a lot.

*Dearest Wondergirl*
*Hope this gets to you before you go away. Well, how did it go? What? Ha ha your intellectual ha ha work experience ha ha again. God, I am in a mature mood tonight. It's because it's the day before my birthday, I guess – did you? I can see you shaking your head. I am not usually like this, am I???*
*Well, school has finished, which is a relief. Then again, I've so much work to do – two art projects and a couple of lovely essays. But I wanted to get a job at the local pub (if my parents will let me and yes, even though I am under age) –*

*not the one down the road, but a bike ride away. I have seen some great blokes serving behind the bar there — know what I mean?*

*It was brill talking to you on the phone the other day. Hope your mobile doesn't damage your brain though. It might have because I could hardly understand what you were saying.*

*So if I said the wrong reply to anything, it was because I couldn't hear properly and was just saying 'yes', 'no', 'it's all right for some', which I usually say to my mum and dad when I'm not listening. Hope you have a great time on holiday. We're going to India for a family wedding, which might be fun though I'll have to behave.*

*How is your 'diet' going? Given up, have you? I can't get through a day without at least one piece of chocolate. I'm sure it's addictive. I'm going swimming every morning to get me and my body fit. Yes — even on the morning of my birthday. Wow Rani, you're a star — how do I do it?*

*My brother's become a real pain — constantly being silly, saying wonderful things like 'Rani, you've got hairs growing out of your chin, just like mummy'. Charming boy — I hate 6-year-olds.*

*Well, wondergirl, I had better send this off — your bestest mate ever*

*Rani xxx*

**19th July** Brenda's passed her driving test. Pete thinks it's her tits that got her through. I hate the way boys talk about girls' breasts behind their backs.

Had a jab at school today against tetanus. Don't know why they couldn't have done it with the measles and rubella jab. I won't need another, and no lock jaw if I cut myself. Should have had it last year, but forgot to give Mum the form to sign (scared of the needle).

Had to line up with all the giggling Year 9s. 'Bet it hurts', 'Suppose I faint?', 'Please, miss, can I have it another time?', 'Could Jane have my one too, please?' 'Cor, look at the size of the needle'. Don't know what the fuss was about. It only hurt if you knocked the injection place a bit afterwards. Had a drop of polio stuff at the same time.

We've got to make our AS level choices tomorrow, when our 6th-form induction course ends. I haven't the faintest idea. Can't really decide till I know my exam results, can I? Pete suggested knitting, animal rights and French – I hope he's failed all his. Mum suggested biology, history and English, and Dad suggested maths, physics and biology…must think I am the 'Brain of Britain' or something.

My physics teacher, Miss Boil, was helpful. She asked me what I thought I wanted to do as a job in the future. I used to want to be a vet during my 'furry animal' stage. During the last 10 years I've wanted to be a racing-car driver, lawyer, woman priest, accountant, computer engineer, business woman, balloonist, explorer, jet pilot, actress, poet, novelist. Now I actually have to make some kind of decision, I can't.

I put myself down for physics, maths, biology, art and English, but can change it later if I want to.

**20th July** School ends today. Pete and Sam are driving up to Scotland in Sam's dad's second car. Some of us hardly even have a first one – Dad's has been on its last legs for 5 years. I'm desperate to go – would even put up with Pete. But 'no no no' from everyone – 'no' from Pete, 'no' from Sam, 'no' from Mum and Dad.

Hate Mum and Dad. I'm 16 now, and anyhow what do they think I'd get up to? Why don't they trust me? I would just have a great time – that's all. And it would be better than some place that Dad's booked on the internet in Wales. It's going to be me, Dad, Gran and Marie, who is due to arrive from France next week.

**29th July** Marie's arrived par train par le Tunnel, et elle says le train was très quick in France and très, très slow in England.

It's not going to be easy. Pete's gone off to Scotland – sharing the driving with Sam, as he's only just got his test. They set off down the road from outside our house at 50 mph, and went screaming round the corner at the end of the street. Dad, who was off to get himself a lottery ticket, wondered whether he should have taken out a life insurance on Pete, because it would be an easier way of making money than his job. Mum called him 'heartless' and burst into tears.

# 11 Summer **Love**?

**1st August** Great summer holiday this:

Scribbling in the back of the car crammed between Gran and Marie, on the way to some wilderness at the back end of nowhere.

Gran's spare teeth in a plastic box on the back shelf of the car and nipping my neck.

Car's broken down twice already.

It's pouring with rain.

NOW stuck in a 5-mile traffic jam on the motorway.

Bovril's been sick and her cat basket stinks.

Marie's sulking because Pete's not coming.

I'm sulking because Marie's coming and Sam's gone with Pete.

Dad's sulking because Gran's coming.

Mum's sulking because Dad's sulking.

Gran hasn't noticed anyone sulking and never stops talking.

And all this for what? – two weeks in a caravan stuck in a caravan site in Barmouth in wet and windy Wales.

Five hours later – and still not there. In fact we're not anywhere as we're lost. Mum insisted on a bit of 'culture' – a visit to Ironbridge, full of things that happened in the Industrial Revolution. Luckily I'd done an essay on it at school. Marie was bored stiff and spent her time in the coffee bar with a 'headache'. Found her chatting up some French-speaking hunk. First words she'd said since we set out.

**2nd August**     Woke snuggled cosily against the ceiling. Bright sun beaming through a chink in the curtains. Bov sitting on my head by my left ear. Pee and flush of Dad in the bog. Lovely smell of Gran making tea and toast – a steaming cup appears at the edge of my bunk. Groan from Mum for us all to shut up please. Marie like a collapsed jellyfish in the bunk opposite.

Just one small problem – I'm on again. Wonder whether Mum and Marie will get it too (Gran must be past it) – all of us living so close together. It's our pheromones again. They cause it – so I read – all of us starting our periods together.

Am lying in my bunk writing this and reading the latest edition of *Cosmopolitan* that Mum disapproves of but still reads from cover to cover herself whenever I buy a copy.

Great not having to get up. Not so great not even being able to fart without the world knowing about it. Doesn't stop Gran gassing off though. Suppose she's got not to mind seeing that she can't control it. I guess you get away with it when you're old. Wish I had packed a gas mask at this very moment – if anyone lights a match the caravan will explode.

Last time I farted it was at home and dead embarrassing because Sam was around and old pompous Pete had to notice and said 'I do detect you're expelling flatus at the distal end of your digestive tract known as your bum. Couldn't you have eructated instead?' As usual, he had to show off and go on about my fart just when I was trying to forget about it. How it was all the air I swallowed because I talked so much and partly it was made up of methane and hydrogen sulphide gas (which was what smelt so bad) from the bugs in my gut working on the food I ate. 'You're just one large walking fart, being a vegetarian and insisting on eating so many beans.' He's a real fart-arse himself – knowing all the answers to everything – but I miss him. Hope he and Sam are OK.

**3rd August** Sun, sun, sun. Marie's got all the gear – sun glasses, three different kinds of sun cream, two beach towels – the lot. Her bikini is about as big as four mouse droppings. Mum's horrified. Keeps saying how it's cold and shouldn't Marie put a jumper on. My bikini looks like an overcoat compared with hers, and I've only got Mum's smelly old hand towel and a bottle of last year's suntan lotion, which seems to have curdled.

We spent the morning lying on the beach. Started with just us, and gradually became surrounded by white spotty bodies, all eyeing Marie, making remarks, and laughing like a herd of nerds. Then Gran arrived with a deckchair, vast knickers and hair bulging out of a bathing cap. She plonked herself down next to Marie, seriously damaging her sexy image.

Old people are really embarrassing sometimes. Not that Gran notices. She completed the picture by starting her knitting. She keeps nodding off – fell asleep in her soup last night. Gran says she can't help it and it's because of her age. Mum and Dad spent the morning in the caravan. Wonder what they're up to?

Marie seems very different from when I was France. Her mum is like a real madame and is very strict about how Marie behaves. Now Marie's here she wants parties and clubbing every night. Hope I'm not going to have to put up with her wingeing and pitying herself all the time.

By evening I was knackered by Marie's sulking and the sun – but still dead white. I'd borrowed Marie's number 50 sun cream. I'm scared of getting skin cancer, especially with the ozone stuff disappearing into some hole over the Arctic, but my white skin is ridiculous. It's got to be down to factor 10 tomorrow. Then I looked at my back in the mirror. Great red streak where I hadn't been able to reach properly with the cream – could even see my finger marks! Just when I wanted to start having a beautiful bronze body.

It's hard work always having to be in the company of someone you don't know very well and don't particularly like and crammed into this space all the time. Marie said she was off for a walk before supper. Some 'walk'! When I went to get milk from the camp shop for Mum, she was being chatted up by the greasy sleazies who were camping on the beach.

It's not that I'm jealous, or even fancy them, but I wouldn't mind some kind of holiday romance myself. Something I can tell Kate and the others about when I get back. After all, a bit of excitement is what holidays are all about. Kate always gets off with some incredibly handsome 20-year-old Porsche driver – or so she says. She lies about her age and thinks you can break all the rules on holiday.

**4th August** Sun. Sun. Sun. Juggling act with Marie's sun screen today. Factor 10 on most of me and factor 50 on the parts which the other screens hadn't reached. Asked Marie to rub it on my back, but one of her admirers flounced over, took the bottle from her and started rubbing it in. I could've sunk into the sand and disappeared with embarrassment, but it was nice at the same time.

The guy's name's Lee. He thinks it's great I'm a vegetarian, as he's a Green. He works as a lab technician in some place near Newcastle. We chatted in the café while Marie disappeared in the direction of the sleazies' tents.

**108**

**5th August** More sun. Met Lee on the beach again. His work's to do with a project measuring the radiation reaching Earth from the Sun. He's into how the chlorine from chloro-fluorocarbons is still damaging the layer of ozone around the Earth in the upper atmosphere. Just one chlorine atom mucks up 10,000 ozone molecules. He seems to know everything about it, and says the ozone layer is important because it mops up ultraviolet light before it reaches the Earth's surface. This ultraviolet-B light is what causes skin cancer and the more that gets through, the more skin cancer people will get.

Lee said the other problem is that people are sunbathing more nowadays. Luckily all the new high-factor sun screens (15 or higher) help cut out the ultraviolet-B light. Most people in hot countries have always known to avoid being out in the summer sun between 11 and 3 o'clock in the day. This is when the sun can do the most harm.

I was getting dead worried till Lee said skin cancer doesn't really happen until we're older. He said I should think about it now though, because if I got a bad sunburn or had too much sun, it would damage my skin and increase my chances of getting skin cancer when I'm older.

Mum is going spare about Marie. She's off all the time with the boys from the tents and Mum doesn't know what to do. Must be worse when you're having to look after someone else's 'little treasure' – as Aunty Pam calls me. Dad was called in to get heavy with Marie. Mum took Gran and me off to the café. I swear I could hear Dad shouting even from there. Marie is red-eyed. All her beautiful make-up was smudged when we got back. Dad said there was no need for me to be smug and I'd better behave or I'd get the same treatment. Total gloom and doom in the caravan. So much for holidays. What am I going to do about seeing Lee?

**6th August** Rain. Has Marie got problems. The latest is spiders. I don't like them, but Marie goes spare. Mum says it's a 'phobia' and wishes it was a 'boy phobia'. A caravan is certainly no place for a holiday if you don't like spiders.

We all sat round telling one another about things people hate. Dad had read that Queen Elizabeth I hated roses. Freud, the headshrink, hated travelling, and King Edward VII wouldn't let anyone mention the number 13. Hans Christian Andersen was afraid of everything. He was so scared of fire that when he stayed in a hotel, he used to sleep with a rope wound around him so that he could escape. He was terrified of dirt too and washed his hands 100 times a day.

Dad thinks it's all silly. In his job he's always meeting people with phobias about mice, rats, wasps, fleas, lice, spiders, beetles – in fact all creepy-crawlies. He's also seen people cured. Apparently what they do is first get them to look at photographs of what they hate – say, spiders. Once they can manage that, they get them to pick up a photo. Then they get them to look at the real thing, stroke it with a pencil, and then actually touch it. I wouldn't fancy touching a tarantula, thanks very much!

Gran had a friend who had what she called 'agoraphobia' because the friend couldn't go out of her house. She got treated in the same way. They took her to the door and just showed her the outside first, then took her for a short distance, and then a little bit more each time she went out.

For Marie, it's not just spiders, she also has a thing about flying. Can't even bear going to the airport, let alone getting on a plane. 'Ze only time I flewed – my 'eart it went boom, boom, boom, I breezed very fast, my fingers zey teengled, my knees zey went to jelly, my skeen it was like a pooool of water.'

Dad's got a phobia because there's 'a great pooool of water' on his bed where the roof is leaking.

**7th August** Rain, rain, rain. Marie and I wanted to spend the day in the café (I haven't seen Lee for two days). But we were dragged off by Mum and Dad for some 'fresh air'. Marie thinks that the 'maladie Anglaise' is having picnics on the beach in freezing cold rain – think I do too. Another Leeless day, but it might have been him whistling at 11.30 p.m. outside. I'm trying not to worry about my exam-results.

**10th August** Sun – and I've managed to see Lee at last. I'd gone with Marie to buy some ozone-friendly insect repellant and he was in the shop. Marie was already making for the tents, so Lee asked if I'd come for a walk on the beach. I thought – why not? Might never get the chance again. You only live once. At least here on holiday I can turn up the sexiness a bit. At home I'd just be called a slag. He may not be the handsomest guy in the world, but he's here, he seems to like me, and he makes me feel good.

We sat (well, a bit more horizontal than sitting) in a hole in the dunes, out of the wind, and told each other about our lives, though I lied about my age and tried to sound experienced. I began to wish I hadn't when things began to get a bit heavy. I wasn't sure just how far to go. I certainly didn't want to go too far. After a while, I began to feel as if it was getting out of control, and I wanted to stay in control, thank you very much. Suddenly I noticed a distant figure. It was Dad, which brought things to an instant halt. All that heavy kissing certainly hasn't spoilt my feelings for Lee – though I'm not sure what he thinks of me now.

Got back to find Gran on the steps of the caravan, shaking out sand from her bri-nylon knickers, which were covered with skidmarks.

If the article I read in Sally's mag is right – that every kiss takes three minutes off your life – I reckon I must be nearly dead by now. Feel exhausted and can't write any more tonight.

Hope Mum and Dad don't notice Marie's love bites, or mine for that matter. We were desperately trying to cover them up with make-up. Nice to have something to laugh about with Marie.

**11th August** Sun, but it might as well be raining because Lee's going today. Saw him in the café. He hadn't told me he was off. He still seems to like me. Don't know what to do now Lee's gone, though he did take my mobile number and said he'd give me a bell. Sun bathing's really pointless. All you do is get brown and then cover it all up because it's too cold. Anyway, people who live in hot countries have really wrinkled skin. I don't want mine to look like Gran's when I'm Mum's age. Mum asked what the matter was. Why does she want me to be happy all the time? I can't be. She isn't.

**14th August** Going home tomorrow. The last few days have really dragged, but Marie's going straight back to France, so I've something to look forward to.

# **Romance** and **Results**

**15th August** Home to Pete. So pleased to see him, even gave him a hug. He pushed me off and told me to stop being emotional, though he was obviously pleased to see me too. Why do boys find it so difficult to show emotion? Hope he's more affectionate with Sandy when he sees her. Bov's OK on emotion. She showed she was pleased to be home by sleeping on my bed last night.

Turns out the boys got stopped for speeding, and breathalysed by an unmarked cop car. Reckon that given all the new cameras they are putting up and the inner-city tolls they are going to charge, it's going to cost a fortune to drive by the time I pass my test. Pete was driving but he never even takes one drink if he's going to drive – he's much too afraid of losing his licence. But he was driving at 83 mph – made me swear not to tell on him to Mum and Dad.

No letter from Lee – surprise, surprise – but maybe I'm expecting too much. Even if I never see him again, he's turned me on to the idea of being a lab technician and doing something useful in life.

Sal's just back from a package holiday to Spain with her girlfriend. Sal's boyfriend couldn't go because he had to work. They won't tell me the details of what they got up to. Said I was too young to know about that sort of thing yet. Must've been good though – they seem all hyped up about it. I told them about my 'romance' with Lee, so they showed me their 'Holiday Romance Survival Kit', which they'd found in a mag on the plane on the way home. Sal said that although the books were right in saying one had to be responsible and considerate, all she wanted to do on holiday was to have a really good time. Felt it was OK, as long as she was careful and took full responsibility for what happened. Here's the article she gave me...

# Holiday Romance Survival Kit

1 Never give away something you might want back, whether it's a gold charm left to you by your grandmother, or your virginity.

2 Beware of moonlight, soft guitar music, sweet words, and cheap red wine – they can all be a headache later.

3 Don't bring anything back with you that you don't want – specially unwanted pregnancies and sexually transmitted diseases. Some of them you'll never get rid of, the worst being Aids.

4 If you might need them, and if you don't know the Italian, Greek, Spanish, Turkish, French or Swedish word for condoms, take some with you. If your memory is bad, you're careless, or just not good at languages – remember emergency contraception. This can be used up to 72 hours after making love, but doesn't protect you against diseases. It is available in most European countries.

5 Never go back to the same place and expect your fantastic hunk to fall into your arms — he'll probably be in somebody else's.

6 Don't expect your feelings, or his, to be the same when you get back home. Holiday romances are holiday romances. One of the definitions of romance is that it's a wild and wanton exaggeration, very remote from the experiences of everyday life.

**16th August** Pete got his exam results today, and lived up to his reputation. Two 'A's and a 'B'. He said what really pissed him off was the 'B', as he'd worked his bollocks off in chemistry but blew the practical — literally, as he set the experiment on fire! He was especially annoyed because Randy Joe got the same results, and appeared to have done no work. Randy thought 'looking as if you worked' had no street cred. Radically cool Sam sent me a postcard! Goodbye Lee, welcome back Sam. Wonder how his exams went?

**20th August** Sandy's back from her hols and I never see Pete. Either he's on the job at M & S or he's on the job with Sandy. He took her to the 'Eye', but I think the view he was looking at from the capsule wasn't London! Mum's getting manky with him. When he's not working, he never helps around the house and only gets out of bed in time to watch *Neighbours*.

**22nd August** Exam results tomorrow. Mum said she'd drive me down to the school.

1 a.m. – can't sleep. Rotten having 'brainy' Pete as a brother. Sure everyone's done better than me. Anyhow, I don't really care because it's not as if me failing my exams is the end of the world. There's a lot else going on in life out there. Mum and Dad have been good about not applying pressure, but I still feel they'd like me to do well and I don't want to let them down.

**23rd August** Crunch time in 10 minutes – must get up. Pete 'greased' me with a 'Don't sweat it honey, have one of mine,' as I left.

Yippee! It was OK – very OK, for me anyhow. All the way there I insisted to Mum that I'd failed everything as a way of protecting myself. Couldn't face going in, so sent Mum instead. She came out looking furious, and I thought 'Oh no – that's it'. Then Mum burst out laughing – 3 'A*'s (for drama, maths and history), 2 'A's (for combined science), 2 'B's, and 1 'U' (for French). At least that wasn't a surprise, though Mum wanted to go for a re-mark. No way.

Kate rang and asked about my holiday. Neither of us could bring ourselves to ask about the other's results, though I was desperate to know hers. Pete said that my results were just because of freaky marking and anyhow GCSEs were getting easier and easier all the time. Don't think he likes competition from his little sister.

Dad's pleased. At least he doesn't think that 'good looks' is all that matters in girls, though boys seem to think different. There was this survey about what boys most admired in girls: (1) good looks (2) understanding (3) warmth (4) honesty (5) loyalty (6) tenderness and only (7) intelligence. Independence, forcefulness and ambition all came last. When it came to what girls admired in boys, it was still good looks at number one. Then: (2) understanding (3) honesty (4) loyalty (5) warmth (6) intelligence.

What was weird was that the same survey showed that what teenagers actually cared about most was (1) cruelty to animals (that would be me two years ago, but now I worry more about pollution and the ozone layer – thanks to Lee, who still hasn't rung or texted) (2) unemployment (3) education (4) famine (5) racial discrimination and (6) nuclear war.

**28th August** A lot of my friends are still away and it's starting to get boring, though I don't want the holidays to end. Everyone is surprised that I did as well as I have – dead insulting of them. Even Mary rang up to congratulate me. Generous of her as she failed three of hers. It's horrible of me, but I feel glad she did badly – she deserved to. She spends all her time out with boys. I know it's awful of me, and I know I'll regret it, but it's just the way I feel right now.

**31st August** Looking forward to seeing all my friends back at school and having a good gossip. Pete's worried because Sandy's dad is back in hospital with some kind of heart problem. He didn't know the right words to comfort Sandy. I suggested he just said how sorry he was to hear about her dad – as long as he said something.

# 13

# **Falling**
to
# **Bits**

**1st September** Still haven't fixed my AS level options. Totally confusing. Why now? I hate making decisions. Seems as if the rest of my life depends on this one.

Back to school in three days. Can't face it. When I get fed up like this, it's usually because I'm tired or bored, or about to have my period, which I am. Looked in the mirror this morning and thought 'God, you look like a frog'. Then thought how pretty everybody else was. When I'm in this mood, I bite Mum's head off – she makes me the maddest. She treats me as if I was a child, and makes comments and jokes that I'd make to a 3-year-old. In her eyes I'm still a little girl, but in mine I'm grown up. I feel like an adult, and I want to make my own decisions without having to consult her first.

Trouble nowadays is that you have the mind of a 20-year-old in the body of a 16-year-old. Mum thinks she's preparing me for a big bad world, but I know as much as she does about life, and in some ways more.

I've decided to write out a list of dos and don'ts for when I become a parent.

**I will:**

>> allow my children to choose whether they do what I want them to do, or not

>> remember what it was like being 16, and try to be more sensitive and understanding

>> be more trusting

>> give them more independence

>> treat them as equals and treat their ideas with respect

>> say sorry to them when I'm wrong

**I will not:**

>> act like a teenager myself

>> be patronizing

>> say things like 'you always…', 'you never…', 'you don't know how lucky you are', 'it's just your age'

>> criticize my children in front of their friends

>> compare them unfavourably with their friends.

**2nd September** Can't write. Totally hopeless. World just full of worries – terrorists, America fighting the world, the environment falling to pieces, Aids everywhere, car pollution, families breaking up, violence – can't stand it.

**4th September** Back to school today. Great to see my friends again. Starting to feel connected.

**5th September** Ouch, itch, scratch, ouch, itch, scratch – the house is hopping with fleas. *Pulex irritans*, Dad calls them. Twenty species attack humans, and it takes one to three weeks for the eggs to hatch after being laid. At least in the UK they don't carry plague or any other nasties. I told Bov how much I hate her because this is all her fault. If only she wasn't so promiscuous. I think fleas should be counted as a sexually transmitted disease. It certainly is with her. I'm bitten all the way from my ankles to my knees, and look a real sight. Mum, Dad and Pete are all scratching.

It's worst when we get back from the summer hols. Dad says it's because the eggs hatch out in the warm wet weather. Of course, the family with a pest control father is the last to get treated. He keeps promising to bring his spray stuff home, but it's always 'tomorrow, tomorrow'. Like my flute practice (which is why I decided to give it up).

If I could have one wish at the moment, I'd wish they'd improve what goes for food at school. It doesn't matter how many times us vegetarians complain, nothing's ever done. I've got the girls on the school council to organize a questionnaire on what everyone eats and what they would like to eat. Now we're in the sixth form, we should have more responsibility.

**6th September** Pete's working at the GAP and is loaded with dosh. He's beginning to worry about going to Nottingham University. He's not so sure he really wants to do medicine. He wishes he'd taken a year off to think about it. Told him that it was because he's afraid of facing real life and hard work…all he said was 'Yes – that's about it!'

I'm still faking it – trying to smile when I'm actually in a deep pit. Can't put the bad things out of my mind. Anyway, I've at last decided on my AS levels. I'm going to do sciences – maths, biology and physics. I got 'A's for those subjects (so much for what Miss Boil said on my report!).

**7th September** Can't face another two years of school, with the same people and the same teachers. Why doesn't anything exciting ever happen in my life?

**8th September** Went round to Emma's. Not there. Her mum says Emma, Kate, Sheila and Mary – MY mates – have gone off to the local shops. Never thought to ask me, did they? Ganging up against me. Pete says I'm being paranoid. Spent afternoon crying and talking to Bov. Got to talk to SOMEONE even if it's only a cat who gives me fleas.

**9th September** My mates came round! Turned out they were buying me a Travis CD yesterday because they thought it would make me feel better. They knew I was having a downer.

We're all going through it. Kate says she's fed up with her body. It's not that she thinks life would be any better if she was slim, but that her head would be less screwed up. If she diets, she only puts it back on again. She can cope with not eating till she gets her period, but then she gets mad cravings. She can be very strict about her eating for a day or so and then something snaps and she stuffs her face with chocolate, chips, sweets, anything fattening. Makes her feel guilty and worthless, and she gets spots and headaches. She wishes she could develop anorexia nervosa, even though she knows it can be a death wish disease. Stupid thing to wish for. From what I read it sounds as if she's getting bulimic though.

Thank goodness I'm happy with myself today and I'm not gross. If others aren't happy, that's their loss. Funny how moods come and go. When Emma felt she couldn't do the work they set her at school last term, she wanted to pack the whole lot in, and leave without taking the exams. Sheila's had it crucially bad. She will have to re-sit some of her GCSEs at evening class, and now she's worried she won't get a job. She nearly got raped and didn't get much support from her parents, and now she feels she can't talk to them about anything.

During the summer Sheila nearly decided to kill herself, like Roger Simpson at St Joseph's School last year. Nobody had realized he was depressed. He seemed to have everything going for him. He sat in his dad's car in the garage with the engine on. Really sad. Everybody felt guilty because they could've done something if only they'd known. After all, Mum says that depression can be treated, just like any other illness.

Sheila rang the Samaritans. Got their number and the Childline one from the local phone book – 0845 790 790 and Childline 0800 1111. She gave them to us – 'You never know', she said. They'd helped her a lot. They'd listened to all her troubles, which made her feel better. They said they got 50,000 calls a year from teenagers, so she wasn't alone. They'd suggested that if she couldn't talk to her parents, she should come and see them. They're open from 8 a.m. till 10 p.m.

I think I might choose to go and see my doctor, especially as she's sent me a leaflet about 'confidentiality'. Says that I can trust my doctor to keep totally private anything I tell her – even if I am under 16. I don't need my parents' permission, and they wouldn't tell my parents if I was having sex (I should be so lucky – Lee, where are you?) or was on the pill – unless I wanted them to know.

Sal came to see me this evening. When she's got nothing better to do, she comes into my room and expects me to amuse her. She'll be nice to me and I'll tell her some of my problems, or talk to her about some boy or other that I fancy. But when her boyfriend's round, she just tells me to push off. If I say anything, she starts getting nasty – telling her boyfriend everything I've told her confidentially.

As it happens, Sal's latest boyfriend's mum works for the Samaritans. It could even have been her on the phone to Sheila. I told Sal about us all being down – Sal's been the same in her time. She'd got some gruesome facts from her boyfriend's mum.

» suicidal thoughts are much more common than threats or actual attempts, and about 1 in 20 boys and about 1 in 10 girls have suicidal thoughts at one time or another.

» actual suicide is rare before the age of 14. After that age about 5,000 teenagers per year attempt suicide, but most of them don't actually want to kill themselves. There are about 130 deaths from suicide among males aged 15 to 19, and 40 deaths among females aged 15 to 19 in England each year, but some of these teenagers didn't mean to kill themselves either – they were just trying to attract attention because they needed help.

> » among all the attempted and actual suicides, there is a definite reason in 2 out of 3 cases, and no clear reason for the others.
>
> » the main reasons for suicidal attempts are: trouble with parents, broken homes, school work, worries about exam failure, fear of unemployment, and relationship problems with a boyfriend or girlfriend. In some cases it is a way of getting away from intolerable stress, and letting other people know how unhappy they are.
>
> » the main feelings that occur before some of the attempts are: anger, feeling lonely or unwanted, worries about the future, and – if depressed as well – feelings of hopelessness.

Sal said that when her friend was very depressed a few years ago, she became real stroppy, bad-tempered, quiet and withdrawn. She was tired all the time, kept bursting into tears, and didn't want to be with anyone. She saw her family doctor and used up all his supply of Kleenex. He arranged for her to see a counsellor, and said that if that didn't help, she might need some tablets to help her get over the depression.

None of this sounded like me. When I get depressed, I listen to my Travis CDs – which Pete says drives HIM to murderous thoughts. I also ring my friends and have a long chat – and going out with my mates or reading a book helps. If I can't do any of those, I sulk till someone notices and have a good moan.

I suppose feelings of sadness are just part of growing up. It's only if they go on for a long time – or get very bad – that one should worry. If mine got very bad, I'd realize I was ill and would go and get some help.

**12th September** We're all into words at school. Words seem to go in and out of fashion like clothes.

### In the 1960s the 'in' words were:

Groovy, fab, ciao, happening, pad, boutiques, far OUT, gear, too good, way out, weird.

### In the 1970s they were:

Hassle, no problem, take care, situation, laid back, zoned, smashed, over the top (OTT), male chauvinist pig (MCP), scene, relate, being INTO something, not my bag, check it out, guy, heavy, trendy, great.

### In the 1980s

Ace, cool, lush, peed off, veg out, gang bang, twat, mellow, chillin, wow, pucker, naff, hip, hunky, horny, posse, dig, groovy, brill, dead cool, fresh, eggy, gross, twerp, bimbo, snog, excellent, wicked, doody, easy, all right, fab, chill out, hot, on the pull, how's it goin?

### In the 1990s

Decent, sound, sorted, safe, kinky, vibes, rude, out to lunch, nice, maca, rude boy, sad, get a life, fit, dodgy, chill, babe, you're a star, hard, threads, sweet, slacker, spinner, rough, rank, stress, mad, shagged out, sucks, weird, get real.

### In 2000

Reckon it was all 'millennium this' and 'millennium that', though 'buff', 'butters', 'rough' and some other stuff seems to have started then.

In 2001 it's a whole lot of other 'street' stuff that people like to use – but most of this comes in and out of fashion faster than my clothes.

Then there's…

## Smart cockney

Know what I mean, bleedin', bloke, dosh, OK mate, right, triffic, down the boozer, ta, dodgy, a right Brian, caff.

## Drug street slang, old and new

Crack, grass, high, trip, billy whizz, speed, blow, ganja, uppers, amphet, snow, coke, smack, henry, skag, gear, score, buzz, ecstasy.

## For those into sex

Copulation, intercourse, fucking, shafting, shagging, bonking, making love, having it off, screwing, making it, doing it, squelching.

## Street cred

It sucks, dude, bad, wicked, yo, sweet, Babylon, def, casual, crucial, dick, ruination, mellow.

God, what do I have to be depressed about? It's ridiculous – the world changes so fast, no wonder I am down one moment and up the next. Did a list of my life:

✩ I have lots of really nice friends

✩ I do look something better than a dish-rag

✩ hardly anyone is REALLY happy at the moment – they just kind of make out they are

✩ Bov loves me

✩ my exam results weren't half bad

✩ my parents really do care about me, even if we do quarrel quite a bit

⭐ I've got an ace brother – even if I hate him sometimes

⭐ I'm better shaped than a balloon

⭐ Sam speaks to me occasionally

What more could I want?

Even if I don't feel totally part of the 'in' crowd and absolutely 'with it' – it doesn't matter. Sal says nobody feels like this anyhow. I bet that the future is going to be absolutely great.

# **Getting Fit** and
# Getting It **Together**

**15th September** There was a txt message on my mobile late this evening – 'CU 2moro at Bodyshack TTFN – Sheila'. I'm worried about her, so txt her back 'RU OK? luv Susie'. Finally gave up when she messaged me back 'ITYFIOK – Sheila'. Didn't understand it – you can have too much of a bad thing, I reckon. So closed down my mobile for the evening and searched the internet for chat rooms instead.

**16th September** Our first day at the Bodyshack keep fit club at the local pool was today. The Samaritans put Sheila on to it. Never dared to go on my own but now we're all going. We were all put through a fitness test before starting and had to answer a load of questions:

1 *Can you walk briskly up and down a flight of 15 stairs three times, and then hold a normal conversation without being out of breath? Yes/No*

2  *Can you do hard running on the spot for 3 minutes without getting tired or short of breath? Yes/No*

3  *Can you quickly step on and off a chair for 3 minutes without getting short of breath? Yes/No*

4  *Can you put your hands flat on the ground with your knees straight? Yes/No*

5  *How many press-ups can you do? 0–5  5–10  10–15  15–20*

They told me I was good on stamina and suppleness but pathetic on strength. I only managed three press-ups. Bit embarrassing as I had said on the questionnaire I could do 10–15. We were lectured by a massive athlete he-woman type who must have been taking male hormones on her cornflakes for the last 10 years, as she was all hairy and muscle-bound. Lecture was on the golden rules of exercise:

1  *Get moving – find more active ways of doing the things you usually do, like running upstairs instead of walking.*

2  *Get fit gradually – it takes time. Make yourself sweaty and out of breath but not uncomfortable.*

3  *Exercise regularly – get into a routine.*

4  *Keep it up – you can't 'store up' fitness.*

5  *Enjoy it – make sure the activities are ones you like and can do regularly.*

We must have been some sight – sitting in the sauna after an hour on the machines. All sweat and flesh, except for Kate, who still looks as if she's come from a Third World drought Aids famine disaster area. I enjoyed it.

Kate was there trying to do away with the remaining 2 kilos of what's left of her body. Sheila was there because the Samaritans said it would take her mind off her unhappiness and her job. She wishes she was still at school, and we wish we had her money. She thought that she would find all the jumping around and being womanhandled by 'men-women' athletes even more depressing – but actually she feels better for it all. Mary was there because she wants to keep her body supple and in shape for the boys, and Emma thinks that if she looks good she's nicer to people.

Nobody there liked us because they're all fatter, flabbier, and well over 40 and think we're taking the piss out of them.

**17th September** Hardly made it out of bed this morning. Don't know how I got to school today. I ache in places I didn't know existed, let alone had muscles in.

**20th September** Am I perverse or perverted? I think I'm becoming a 'Fitness Freak'. Haven't really thought about sport since I twisted my ankle before the 400 metres (when I was 13). Now I'm in the lower sixth where my teachers tell me I don't have to do it – I want to. But I don't want to do weedy little girls' sports like rounders and netball – childish, boring, tedious, and with too many rules. I want to do violent sports like rugby – rampaging around the field getting really dirty, smashing people to the ground, and basically beating up anything that moves. Then going off and getting all pink and clean in a shower and feeling really good afterwards.

Where can girls play rugby, except at posh schools costing £13,000 a year? I wonder why blokes like team sports and seem more competitive than women. Must be something to do with their genes giving them macho hormones. Or maybe it was being brought up by mums and dads expecting them to be like that. I love competing as long as I win – otherwise it's dead boring.

Pete's a total pain, letting everyone down all the time and never doing what he promises to do. He thinks he's 'in love' with Sandy. I think he's being stupid. He promised to come with Kate and me to the late night cinema yesterday. Mum said we couldn't go otherwise, in case we got attacked. I sometimes think Mum is being overprotective. Just because I'm a girl she thinks I'm automatically going to get mugged or raped or something. Pete was allowed out at night by himself at my age. Then Sandy rang and asked Pete to go to the pub, and he rushed off to see her, so we couldn't go.

He's not going to have any friends left when it finishes between him and Sandy. He keeps letting them down. Kate and I told him girls hate boys who are doormats. Personally I don't think it's love – I think it's sex – but I reckon maybe sex can be a religion for some people.

**23rd September** A session on the torture rack but I'm definitely getting fitter. We were lectured again by the hairy-bottomed monster – on the exercise value of the different sports:

**Walking** – *great for stamina but not so good for suppleness and strength. For all-round fitness, you need another sport as well.*

**Swimming** – *excellent for strength, suppleness and stamina, especially if you use various strokes.*

**Cycling** – *great for stamina and leg strength, but not so hot on suppleness.*

**Jogging and running** – *a fun, free and quick way to get fit. Good for stamina but not so good for suppleness.*

**Badminton** – *fun even for beginners. Good for stamina, flexibility and strength.*

**Tennis** – *fun and sociable, and good all-round exercise.*

**Squash** – *very exercising, providing good all-round activity. Warm up before you start.*

**Team games** – *great for stamina and strength, and pretty good for suppleness. You don't have to be good to play.*

**Weight training** – *helps tone up your body and keep you slim and supple.*

*The ideal is to do 30 minutes exercise 5 times each week to make you sweat — any kind. But even if you can't do this much, some is better than none.*

It seems you have to do an awful lot of exercise to work off the calories you put on by just drinking one pint of full-fat pasteurized milk. To do that, madam said you'd have to:

> walk for 76 minutes
> swim normally for 60 minutes
> walk fast for 54 minutes
> play badminton for 48 minutes
> run slowly for 47 minutes
> cycle for 46 minutes
> play tennis or do aerobics for 42 minutes
> run fast or swim fast for 32 minutes
> play squash for 22 minutes

Pete said that making love was the equivalent exercise of running a mile. Wonder how he knows, don't reckon he's done it yet.

We did weight-lifting this week. I think the weights I lifted weighed more than Kate. Kate herself looked like a bent beanpole holding up Big Ben. Sheila's flagging. She thinks horse-riding is more her style. She likes the feeling of power and control and being taller and looking down on people. She also likes the 'Jilly Cooper' romantic image.

**24th September** Beginning to get upset again about Lee still not making contact, and Sam's about to disappear from my life. He's off to work his way round the world. He certainly won't be interested in ME after adventures in hot countries filled with glamorous, sexy women.

There's too much pressure nowadays over having a boyfriend. Everyone seems to expect you to and when you don't, you begin to wonder what's wrong.

It feels like I'm beginning to lose my confidence and get depressed again. It starts with one thing, like whether I've got any friends, and goes on to another – my looks, my clothes. Everything begins to crumble. I always seem to be comparing myself with my friends. Want to break out and be original but I can't. How can I explain it? It's at times like this that actually I really appreciate Pete being around. Even if we argue all the time, having a brother is like having a really good extra friend, and it gives me a good feeling of security.

**25th September** Bicycling to school's more fun now I'm fitter. I beat speedy Winston up the hill today. The good thing about cycling is that if you're not feeling competitive you can go at your own speed, and see things you don't see otherwise. The bad thing is the danger, I suppose. I'd wear a crash helmet if it didn't make me feel that I look real sad. Think the only way they'll get people to wear them is by making it compulsory.

**26th September** Pete's out with Sandy again. He's meant to be getting things ready for university but seems to have a one-track mind. A whole gang of them are going to another gig, as if the Reading festival wasn't enough. They had a long pep talk from Sam's dad about the dangers of drugs. He said the police and the pushers would be out in force – and not to expect him to come and bail them out. As usual – I'm NOT allowed to go.

Sam's dad gave us all photocopies of an article on drugs. Typical that I'm given the menu and not allowed to go to the feast. Anyhow, here it is:

---

# Warning – drugs and being involved with the police can be harmful to your health

## Remember – you don't have to join the drug scene

*CANNABIS (weed, green, dope, grass, ganja, hash, marijuana, etc.) Commonest illegal drug in the UK. Comes in different forms: as a resin which is smoked or cooked in food, or as a leaf which is smoked with tobacco. Effects include relaxation and making your senses (taste, hearing, sight) more acute. Doesn't cause a hangover and is probably not addictive. Does, however, reduce concentration, makes short-term memory worse, and very occasionally can cause acute confusion. People who smoke it all the time aren't called 'dope heads' for nothing. Other bad effects are that if you already have, or are susceptible to, mental problems, it can make them much worse; and smoking cannabis has many of the same long-term dangers as smoking tobacco.*

*ECSTASY (E, MDMA, ice, XTC, discobiscuits) Gets you up to 7 years for possession. Known as the 'rave' drug and is being*

---

used by thousands and thousands of people. Peddled as a safe and OK drug – which it is NOT – and most of what is sold as ecstasy contains aspirin, dog-worming pills, and a million other substances as well. The effects of genuine E (if anyone ever gets any!) are to make users friendly, energetic and generally feel delighted with their lot. Can also sometimes cause mild dizziness and nausea. What's really worrying is what damage ecstasy can do to your brain and liver in the long run. It also can cause the occasional death among people using E, which appears to be associated with the drug giving you the impression that you can 'rave' for ever. This leads to exhaustion and dehydration due to sweating so much – and that can cause sudden death.

**AMPHETAMINES** (speed, uppers, sulphate, whizz, billy) Up to 5 years for possession. Made artificially and like E is usually sold with a whole lot of other crap in it. Sniffed, swallowed, smoked or injected – but injection is very, very risky. Sniffing damages your nose, and rubbing it into your gums makes your teeth fall out. Makes you feel powerful, self-confident and energetic. In the long run, the effects of using the drug are tiredness, depression, and acute feelings that people are getting at you – quite apart from the damage it does to your body.

**LSD** (acid) Up to 7 years for possession. Trips absolutely terrible or wonderful, partly dependent on your mind state when you take it, but some people do go really peculiar on it and never get right again. Very occasionally people have jumped out of windows and done very foolish things while on it. Totally artificially made substance giving you an 'out of body' experience. Effects can take 24 hours or longer to wear off. Can cause acute anxiety.

**COCAINE and CRACK** (coke, charlie, snow, freebase, rock, wash) Up to 7 years for possession. Crack is a popular form of cocaine. Both are nasty, exceedingly addictive drugs. The effects (very fast and short with crack) make you feel really great. You need and want more and more to get that great feeling back. If you have to do drugs – DON'T do crack.

**HEROIN** (skag, junk, smack, gear, brown) Up to 7 years for possession. Comes from the poppy – but not the kind you get in Britain. Smoked, sniffed or injected. Often very impure. Makes you feel relaxed, happy and content when you take it. Highly addictive and difficult to get off. You feel rotten when you can't get it and want more and more of it. It's another drug NOT to do even if someone tries to persuade you it's OK just to try once. If you do try it, never use a needle used by anyone else, as that's the way Aids and hepatitis get spread.

**GLUE AND GAS SNIFFING** Not at all a good scene. Causes two deaths a week in the UK and the threat of brain, liver and kidney damage. There are more than 30 substances around which give you an altered state of mind through sniffing. One of the main dangers is doing something really stupid while under the effects.

Remember again:

## If you do experiment – know what it's all about

## At all costs stay away from injecting: the drugs are likely to be impure and you are highly at risk of getting Aids and a nasty liver disease called hepatitis

**27th September** I've lost the key of my cycle lock, so I left my bike at school and walked.

Pete's gig trip nearly ended with them all in jail. Turned out Sam's doctor dad had forgotten to take his medical bag, containing drugs like heroin and morphine, out of the car. The police had stopped Sam near the concert for a routine check. The sniffer dogs were just about to start in when a psychedelic van whizzed past and got stopped and searched instead. It wasn't till they got back that they realized what a near miss it had been!

Pete said that there were dealers everywhere, sidling up all the time, trying to sell crack. He wanted to smash their faces in.

**28th September** Still no bike but I have the key. Found it this evening in Bov's basket. How did it get there?

**29th September** Bike, key and lock all together at last. Collected bike from school in spite of the fact it's Saturday. Pete tore himself away from Sandy to drive me down in Dad's car.

All my pals are coming round this evening for a 'gathering'. (No, Mum – it's not a party.)

**30th September** Was struggling out of bed to go to the keep fit club – aerobics this week – when heard sudden scream of anger from Mum. She'd cracked at last…she started with:

Who the hell were the couple sleeping in the hall in a sleeping bag?

Why were there cigarette burns on the dining-room table?

Why was there broken glass by the back door?

Why was the milk still out of the fridge?

Why was there no bread left?

Why had all the lights been left on downstairs?

Why was the downstairs loo blocked with paper?

Why was the kitchen floor covered with crisps?

Who had drunk Dad's bottle of Jack Daniels?

Why was the sink full of washing-up?

Why was the back door left unlocked?

Why were there three strange bicycles in the back garden?

Why was the house such a pigsty?

Thought she'd never stop but Pete made things worse by asking Mum what her problem was. Thought she was going to hit him, but he's bigger than she is now.

Never made it to aerobics, unless you count clearing up at home as aerobic exercise. Mum said I'm not missing anything as long as I take some exercise and today she'd rather it was at home – thank you very much.

# **Death,**
# **Dreads** and Drama

**1st October** Pete's in the dumps, getting at me and the world in general. He referred to the human race as a 'foul genetic mistake'. Think that American terrorist thing in NY is still on his mind, though it is way past. I asked him and he told me to 'grow up'. Said being mature wasn't only being aged 16, being able to make love legally, making decisions about A and AS level choices, and being able to have a conversation of more than three sentences. He thinks that his extra two years' experience makes all the difference. He's so patronizing.

Anyhow, he and Sandy are pathetic – going around together like an old married couple.

**2nd October** SANDY'S DAD HAS DIED. Wish I hadn't written that stuff in my diary yesterday. He had another really bad heart attack yesterday. Pete's in a state and doesn't know what to do. Whether to ring up, whether to go to the hospital, whether to go and see Sandy at home, and what to say to her and her mum. Mum says he must go and see her. There's nothing worse than people avoiding you when disaster happens. That's what friends are for – to be there.

Pete came back later. He said Sandy had cried a lot but had been really pleased he'd come. Him just being there had helped her, even though it was a bit awkward at first. Sandy doesn't seem to believe it's happened. She still expects her dad to walk in at any moment. Pete wants to talk about it. It feels so different from when Jason's dad died last year. Pete had found Jason in the pub the same evening, as though nothing had happened. Strange, the way different people react totally differently to someone dying.

**5th October** The idea of Mum and Dad dying frightens me. Don't think I slept all night, worrying about it.

Pete went to Sandy's dad's funeral. He's sure that funerals are a good thing – sort of marking the fact for everyone that the person has died, and is being buried and not allowing all those fantasies about the person still being alive. Not that he'd enjoyed going to the church, but he was able to say some sort of 'goodbye'. Even Sandy's younger brother, aged 5, had been at the cremation. I think Pete's right because I still don't quite feel Grandad's gone. His was a heart attack too. I keep seeing people who look like him, and my heart sort of sinks each time.

In spite of all the sadness, Pete looked a real laugh going off in Dad's dark suit, Sam's too-big black shoes, and awful Uncle Bob's black tie.

Pete's getting himself a donor card. He doesn't want to be flattened by a passing car without being useful to the human race. There are hundreds of people waiting for kidney transplants, corneal eye transplants and heart transplants (and I should be waiting for a brain transplant, he reckons). Once he's dead, he doesn't care what happens to his body. He gets angry with me when I say I don't want to have doctors arranging for bits of me to be walking about inside other people when I die. He thinks I'm really selfish not to carry a card and that everyone should agree to help other people. Still not sure I like the idea of my kidneys washing out pee in somebody else's body, but I do understand that donating bits of you may save someone else's life though.

Couldn't sleep again. Came down at 2 a.m. to make Ovaltine, and found Pete with the downstairs phone glued to his ear and falling about laughing. I was worried he'd wake Mum and Dad. He couldn't sleep either (he called it 'insomnia') and was trying all these numbers he'd found in a magazine. So far he'd found all this recorded information on:

*What is an orgasm?*

*Masturbation – the facts*

*Is it wrong for me to dream about sex?*

*Can love just be lust?*

Almost all the numbers had been engaged. Now I know what insomniacs do at 2 a.m. All Pete could get through to was 'Girls' Bodies'. Couldn't think why he was laughing, so when he'd finished I rang the 'Boy's Bodies' number and discovered. A disembodied voice told me of all the 'hidden treasures' I could find inside boys' boxer shorts. What a load of crap. As for masturbation, one of Mum's magazines says that 90% of boys admit to doing it and the other 10% are liars, and it seems that a lot of girls do it too!

**6th October** Exhausted. Pete insists that he's just the same as Napoleon, Margaret Thatcher and Churchill, and can manage on 4 hours' sleep a night. Hadn't noticed it myself, given the difficulty he has getting up in the morning.

Pete had another go at Dad about smoking today. It worries him that Dad might get cancer or have a heart attack. At least he's not smoking as many cigarettes as he used to.

I don't think I'll have any more arguments with Mum and Dad. What if they died suddenly and I was never able to make it up to them?

**7th October** Held my older brother's hand when we drove him up to his university in Nottingham today! I knew he needed me as Sandy couldn't go, but he gave the impression of wanting to get rid of me and Mum as soon as we were there.

I want to go to university. There are condom machines in all the loos, so life there must be wild, I reckon. Think Dad tried to give Pete a packet before we left, as there was a sort of scuffle in the hall with Pete looking dead offended and muttering something about getting his own if he needed them, thanks very much.

**9th October** Sandy came round. I think that she was missing Pete. I was terrified I might giggle out of nervousness, so I gave her a big hug. She burst into tears and I knew I was going to sob too. She's having to be strong, and trying not to cry in front of her mum. Being the eldest, she feels she has to be responsible and support her. She said she keeps wondering what she's done wrong in life to deserve her dad dying like that.

**10th October** Got smashed by Emma at squash today, but it was a good game. Sandy's dad's death has made us all a bit down. While banging around the squash court, Kate told me that she had had a sister who died from something called meningococcal meningitis when Kate was 5. She's never talked about it before because her parents never explained what happened, and now they tried to pretend that her sister had never existed. Kate had gone through sheer hell when it happened, and no one could cheer her up or could understand what she was going through. Her parents had said 'Time will heal'. Although that was true, it had been the last thing she had wanted to hear then. She remembered one day when one of her friends had tickled her to cheer her up. Instead of laughing, like she usually did, she had burst into tears, and everyone had felt dead embarrassed...oops, maybe that's the wrong word.

**11th October** Sandy's back at school. We're trying to be really nice to her, and really considerate, but some people just don't know how.

**12th October** It's like when I had my exams. I'm not sleeping a wink at night and I'm even missing Pete....never thought that would happen. Mum's sympathetic and says lots of things can cause being so depressed, like anxiety, stress, overwork, or sadness at someone dying. Dad says that most people who think they haven't slept a wink have been found in experiments to actually go to sleep 20 minutes after going to bed, and then to sleep for a good 6 hours. Trouble is, that's not the way it feels to me. I lay awake all last night, worrying I was not going to get to sleep.

**14th October** Still not sleeping properly. Mum said she'd find me something from the doctor's to read about not being able to get to sleep, and that sleeping tablets at my age were not the best answer, as they can become addictive if you start taking them too often.

At least I've got Bov to keep me company and she and I really understand one another. She never answers me back, unlike some people in this house. She's been 'my' cat since Sal moved out. I sometimes wonder whether I would mind her dying more than a human.

**15th October** Terrible noises outside last night. Doesn't help my sleep problem, being scared to death. I decided it was Dad snoring, till I looked in the garden this morning. Bov's killed Pinko. I'm going to kill Bov next time I see her. Why can't cats be vegetarians?

Pinko went into the ground at the bottom of the garden alongside the other eight graves – two hamsters, three rabbits, a mouse, a gerbil and Gran's budgie. Had to be careful with the grave-digging as I wasn't sure what manky remains I might come across.

I hope cemeteries are more organized. Personally, I don't fancy being cremated. Bit like being charcoal-grilled and ending up as a little pile of grey ashes like Sandy's dad. I want to go into the ground whole – like Pinko. Dad disagrees and thinks that it is ridiculous using large parts of the countryside for burying the dead.

**16th October** At last Mum's got the stuff on how to get to sleep. My Thought for the Day is 'Does everybody tear the cardboard roll of the toilet paper and use it when the paper has run out? If the answer is 'yes', then why don't they make the centre bit softer so it doesn't hurt one's bum so much?' Here's what the article in the paper said.

144

# TIPS FOR NON-SLEEPERS

The bit of your body that most needs sleep is your brain. Everything from your neck down can do without it, provided it gets regular rest and food. Even your brain, on average, only needs 6 hours' sleep a night, but this varies very much from person to person.

There appear to be two main kinds of 'sleep' – 'vital' or 'deep' sleep and 'optional', 'light' or 'rapid eye movement' sleep (because your eyes move rapidly backwards and forwards behind your closed eyelids). The second kind of sleep is when you dream, the first kind is the kind that revitalizes your brain. 'Short sleepers' are able to miss out on 'optional' sleep but not on 'vital' sleep. Feelings of 'sleepiness' are what finally tell us whether we are getting enough sleep or not.

Some things to do to help you to sleep:

1 Accept that *whatever* sleep you can get is going to be really enjoyable.

2 Try to go to bed at a regular time every night, and set your alarm for the morning so that you don't get anxious about waking up on time.

3 Don't indulge in weekend sleep binges.

4 Try relaxation exercises, or a brisk walk, in the hour or so before you go to bed.

5 Don't indulge in heavy meals, Coca-Cola, alcohol, tea or coffee (unless decaffeinated) just before going to bed.

6 It's worth trying to drink a glass of warm milk, hot chocolate or Ovaltine before going to bed.

7 Make sure your mattress and pillows are comfortable and the bedroom is not too hot or cold.

8 Have a pee before going to sleep.

9 If you can't get to sleep, don't toss and turn – get up and go and do something in another room. You don't want to associate your bedroom with sleeplessness.

10 Try relaxation tapes that are available in some shops like Boots.

# 16 I've **Got** to Have It

**17th October** Something had changed when I woke up this morning. I'd slept! Waking was like swimming to the surface of a deep, dark pool – up and up and up to sunlight shining through the window. Maybe it's because I think I just might have a boyfriend, at least I hope I have. I'll wait before I write his name down – things might just go wrong.

**18th October** I'm fed up with being an only child at home. Was down the local newspaper shop buying *J-17* and met Dad buying a scratch-card National Lottery ticket. If it was me and I won £12,000,000, I'd buy Sam's body for my own personal use, Dad a Merc, Mum a trip to a health farm, and I'd give most of the rest to Oxfam and Save the Children.

**19th October** Our food 'questionnaire' has worked. The school's into 'NEW-LOOK, HEALTHY EATING', with a typical, massive 'Let's all do this together' type programme. There's a word search in the school magazine, and even the dinner ladies are involved (they're fed up with making custard and jam pudding).

| F | W | H | O | L | E | M | E | A | L | B | B | D | P |
|---|---|---|---|---|---|---|---|---|---|---|---|---|---|
| N | V | O | T | Z | N | P | E | A | S | A | R | O | C |
| U | L | E | N | T | I | L | S | F | A | N | O | U | E |
| N | K | T | G | O | T | F | A | P | P | T | W | G | L |
| S | C | P | C | E | U | F | I | S | H | A | N | N | E |
| A | H | U | E | Q | T | L | C | B | U | A | B | B | K |
| T | O | L | P | A | B | A | F | S | R | N | R | O | Y |
| U | N | L | E | W | R | N | B | O | I | E | E | T | C |
| R | L | E | Q | R | K | U | E | L | C | L | A | T | R |
| A | A | T | O | M | A | T | O | C | E | D | D | L | I |
| T | F | T | D | A | P | O | T | A | T | O | P | N | S |
| E | T | U | H | T | P | L | U | M | S | M | I | N | K |
| D | E | C | A | Z | L | C | C | E | R | E | A | L | U |
| A | K | E | L | P | E | K | I | L | S | E | U | M | T |

The boys on the school council hate us, though, and have been to see the head. They even arranged for the local chip van to visit at 12.30. Maybe it's because it sells fags as well.

I'm really proud of our survey. We got the whole sixth form to think out the questions, give out the questionnaire, and analyse the answers on one of the school computers. Only blot on the landscape was the questionnaire that we gave to the staff. They won't let us analyse that – will they?

## Analysis of 'Healthy Eating' questionnaire

### Question 1

(a) Do you think the food provided by the school is healthy?

Yes – 40%      No – 60%

(b) Do you consider the food you eat at home is healthy?

Yes – 80%    No – 20%

## Question 2

What are your favourite foods?

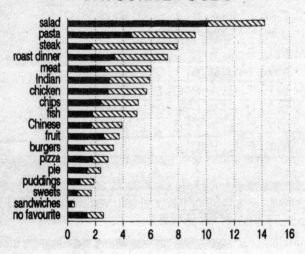

### FAVOURITE FOODS

girls

boys

## Question 3

Are your favourite foods available at school?

Yes – 20%    No – 80%

## Question 4

How often do you eat chips?

**CHIP CONSUMPTION**

## Question 5

How many portions of fruit and/or vegetables do you eat in a day?

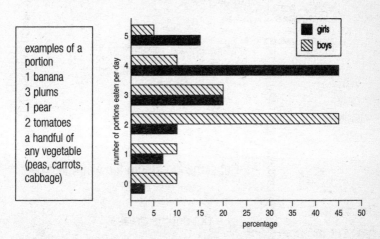

examples of a portion
1 banana
3 plums
1 pear
2 tomatoes
a handful of any vegetable (peas, carrots, cabbage)

The survey showed that girls are better at eating fruit and vegetables than boys. Only 5% of boys and 15% of girls eat the ideal of 5 portions of fruit or vegetable a day.

# Other Comments You Have about Health and Food in School

What about us vegetarians? Let's have more variety – instead of salad and a lump of cheddar cheese.

Less lumps in the custard please.

They shouldn't let local shops sell fags.

Raise the age you can buy fags to 18.

Why was Doreen's toe-nail in my salad?

Why do all dinner ladies look like jam rolls?

Lots of fruit but no tarantulas please.

Unbruised apples please.

Tidying the school up might help.

Can we have more chips please?

Why only white rolls?

More choice please – what about Indian and Chinese food?

Get someone to turn the water into beer.

Cut out the grease!

Why can't we have more West Indian food, man?

Don't eat the food.

Glad it's worked. We now have baked potatoes, wholemeal rolls, vast salads of every variety, and nice fresh fruit. Dinner ladies don't look any thinner though – think they are going out for chips like most of the boys! Also found a great '5 pieces of fruit and veg a day' poster, which we've put up all over the school.

**21st October** OK – his name is 'Willie' (not a joke). He's fit and about 6 foot tall, blond-haired, very attractive, in the upper sixth, wears really cool shirts, smells great and apparently is a good kisser and dancer, though Sandy says he's a bit of a stud.

Thank goodness Pete's away and doesn't know about him or he'd be into remarks like 'willie by name, willie by nature' – that sort of thing. Anyhow Willie has started coming to the Sports Centre on Sundays and we walk home together, but my friends are always with us. He says he'll help me babysit for my next-door neighbours on Tuesday.

**23rd October** 'Thought for the Month' – I HATE MEN…really bad attack of 'boy rage', or more specifically 'Willie rage'. They only think of one thing. I got Mum and Dad's permission for Willie to come and babysit with me at Mrs Smith's. Dad gave me a lecture on 'reputation' and stuff. Because I'm the youngest he can be very protective.

Anyway, Willie came round and after the children had all gone to sleep, we sat on the sofa and snogged for quite a long time. Then he pushed me onto the floor and asked me to have sex with him! I said 'NO' –

though deep down I quite wanted to. I really fancied him, but I've only known him for two weeks. He kept on and on about it, but I still said 'NO'. He asked me 'Why not?' I told him that it wasn't that I was scared, but that I'd never done it before, wasn't about to now, and at my age didn't want to risk getting pregnant. He gave me some bull about boys under the age of 18 not being able to get a girl pregnant – he must have thought I was really thick and piss-easy. He also can't have read my article on sex and contraception in the school newspaper. He must know the facts – he's been to the same sex education classes at school as I have. By my reading of the stuff, most boys have active sperm at 13. Said he wouldn't pack me in, and that he really loved me. Yeah, I thought, keep talking. But I wasn't going to give in, and in the end he left.

After he'd gone, I was furious. Being a virgin means something to me. I'm not just going to throw it away with ANYONE.

**25th October** Willie got his sister to phone and tell me that he didn't want to go out with me any more. I didn't feel upset. I knew he'd do something like that. I was just really angry he hadn't had the guts to tell me to my face. At school he's spreading rumours that I'm tight and can't kiss, and says he isn't going to bother with a frigid cock-teaser like me. Boys like that just aren't worth knowing. Sleep with a guy, you're a slag – don't sleep with him, you're frigid.

I told Mary a bit about it – though not the details! My friends have nicknamed him 'Mini Willie'. They say he's probably got his big muscles, not because he exercises, but because he used anabolic steroids like they do in the Olympics – even though anabolic steroids give you 'deformed genitals'.

**26th October** No lock, no bike now – just a key. Daren't tell Mum as I never got round to buying the combination lock. Just said I felt like a walk. 'It's good exercise, Mum.'

Geek at school, who's self-appointed leader of the 'chip and fag' gang, came up to me in the common room and said: 'I don't believe what you say about fatty foods giving you a heart attack when you're older. My grandad is 85 and has always eaten lots of greasy food, and smoked 20 fags a day.' I told him to clean out his ears. What I had said was not that fatty foods and smoking WILL give you a heart attack, but that eating fatty foods and smoking makes you much more LIKELY to get a heart attack.

I thought Mum would have a heart attack when I got back and told her about the bike. But she already knew! How do they always know before you even tell them?

Dad came in this evening looking as if he was a cat who'd swallowed the cream. He's won £2000 on a lottery scratch card and reckons we should all go and have a weekend in Paris!! Can't believe it. Never thought anyone won anything on them.

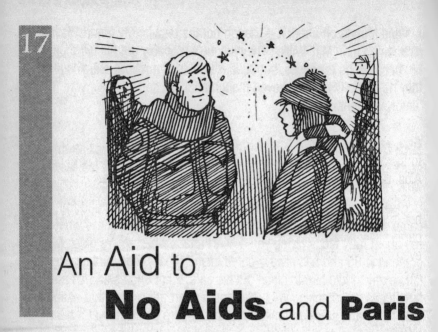

# An Aid to
# **No Aids** and **Paris**

**2nd November** What is it about me and boys? I don't know, but I am NOT going to worry – it's the boy's problem not mine. Dad's taking the whole family to Paris with his lottery winnings. Great but can't believe it. He's booked it all on the internet for next weekend.

**5th November** Nobody's having their own fireworks this year. Too many accidents in past years, and anyway Dad says fireworks cost too much.

Went to the public fireworks in the park instead. Spotted John with Charlie in the crowd. Hadn't set eyes on Charlie for nearly 5 months!

I nudged Kate – who dropped her toffee apple in the mud. I didn't think they'd seen us, till I heard John shouting my name. Charlie didn't seem to want to look at me. He explained that he'd lost my phone number, and that HE was waiting for ME to phone HIM.

**6th November** Last week some trendy doctor gave out a questionnaire to the sixth form. Said she wanted to know what we knew and felt about Aids. Everybody else scribbled away, so reckoned they knew it all.

Sita Beegam's parents wouldn't let her fill it in. She's really nice, but her family won't allow her to do any of the things which we're doing, like parties or questionnaires about Aids. She isn't allowed out in the evenings at all, and her parents won't even allow her to attend PSHE lessons, let alone the school Christmas party. Sita knows her parents are like that because they were brought up that way, and they think it is best for her too – but she doesn't think they understand what it is like nowadays. How is she meant to learn about relationships and sex and stuff?

Anyhow, here's the questionnaire the doctor gave out, which luckily wasn't about my private life – given I don't have one…

# What do you know about Aids?

PLEASE FILL IN THIS QUESTIONNAIRE

The answers will be given to you later

**How old are you?** .......years .......months

**Which sex are you?** male        female

1 What does A......I......D......S...... stand for?

2 What causes Aids?

3 What does H.........I.........V.........stand for?

4 When was Aids first discovered?

   1950–1960?   1960–1970?   1970–1980?   After 1980?

5 How and where did it start?

6 Roughly how many people in the UK have the Aids disease?

   1,000     5,000     10,000     100,000

7 Roughly how many people in the UK have already died from Aids?

   50     1,000     5,000     7,000     13,500

8 If you get the Aids virus, is there a test that can be done straightaway that will show you whether you have got it?

Yes / No / Don't know

9 If you get infected with the Aids virus, does the infection last for the rest of your life?

Yes / No / Don't know

10 If you get infected by the Aids virus, do you get ill with it immediately?

Yes / No / Don't know

11 Do all people infected by the Aids virus die from it?

Yes / No / Don't know

**12 How do you know that you have got the Aids disease?**

**13 Is there a cure for Aids?**
Yes / No / Don't know

**14 Can the Aids virus be passed on even if you don't know you have it?**
Yes / No / Don't know

**15 In a person who has been infected by the Aids virus, where will the virus be?**

| | |
|---|---|
| in their skin | Yes / No / Don't know |
| in their faeces (shit) | Yes / No / Don't know |
| in their saliva (spit) | Yes / No / Don't know |
| in their semen (sperm) | Yes / No / Don't know |
| in their tears | Yes / No / Don't know |
| in their urine (pee) | Yes / No / Don't know |
| in their blood | Yes / No / Don't know |
| in their vagina | Yes / No / Don't know |

**16 How can a person catch the Aids virus?**

| | |
|---|---|
| by touching doorknobs | Yes / No / Don't know |
| by sharing dishes and glasses | Yes / No / Don't know |
| by sharing toothbrushes | Yes / No / Don't know |
| by sharing needles to inject drugs | Yes / No / Don't know |
| by using lavatory seats | Yes / No / Don't know |
| by giving the 'kiss of life' | Yes / No / Don't know |
| by wet (French) kissing | Yes / No / Don't know |
| by droplets of saliva | Yes / No / Don't know |
| by anal intercourse | Yes / No / Don't know |
| by holding hands | Yes / No / Don't know |

by touching an infected person's blood    Yes / No / Don't know

by blood transfusion    Yes / No / Don't know

by head lice    Yes / No / Don't know

by mother to unborn baby    Yes / No / Don't know

by drinking breast milk    Yes / No / Don't know

by sneezing and coughing    Yes / No / Don't know

by vaginal intercourse    Yes / No / Don't know

**17 When having sex...**

can a man catch the Aids virus from an infected man?

Yes / No / Don't know

can a man catch the Aids virus from an infected woman?

Yes / No / Don't know

can a woman catch the Aids virus from an infected man?

Yes / No / Don't know

can a woman catch the Aids virus from an infected woman?

Yes / No / Don't know

**18 Give the three groups of people you think are most at risk of catching the Aids virus:**

a) ...........................

b) ...........................

c) ...........................

**19 Which of the following kills off the Aids virus outside the body?**

heat    Yes / No / Don't know

soap and water    Yes / No / Don't know

disinfectants    Yes / No / Don't know

**20 If you have sex with a condom, does it protect you against getting Aids?**

Yes / No / Don't know

**21 If you had a friend who was worried about Aids, where do you think he/she should go first for help? (circle one only)**

casualty department of local hospital    family doctor

family planning clinic    school nurse

sexually transmitted disease clinic    teacher

Aids telephone 'help' line    parents

friends

**22 Write the numbers 1 to 4 against the things which worry you most – in the order that you find them most worrying (1 against the most worrying, 2 against the next most worrying, and so on) – among the following:**

failing your exams

leaving home as a young man or woman

catching Aids

a parent or brother or sister dying

a terrorist attack

being out of work

having an argument with your parents

being arrested for using drugs

not having a 'steady' friend of the opposite sex

your favourite pet dying

What a sweat filling this in – sure I got half the answers wrong. The doctor gave us out the answers afterwards…

# Aids – All Your Questions Answered

## 1 What does 'AIDS' stand for?

'Acquired Immune Deficiency Syndrome'. It was given this name because the effect of the disease is to destroy the body's normal defences (immune system) to infections.

## 2 What causes Aids?

A virus. Most Aids infections are caused by a virus called HIV1. Researchers have found another virus that causes Aids called HIV2, and others are being discovered.

## 3 What does 'HIV' stand for?

'Human Immunodeficiency Virus', because it affects the body's immune system.

## 4 When was Aids first discovered?

It was first noticed in America in the early 1980s. However, there was one case in America in the 1970s of a boy who died from a mysterious and previously unknown disease. They saved some of his blood, and when they tested it in the 1980s they discovered that he might have been infected with the Aids virus.

## 5 How and where did it start?

We don't really know, but it may have come from a person coming into contact with a certain kind of 'green' monkey in Africa. It is then said to have spread to America via one airline steward who had many sexual partners.

## 6 How many people in the UK have been diagnosed with the Aids disease?

By the end of 2000, the number of Aids cases had reached 17,000, with 41,000 diagnosed with HIV.

## 7 How many of these people have died from Aids?

By the end of 2000 at least 13,500 people had died from Aids in the UK. 36 million people in the world are thought to be infected with the Aids virus. Over 15 million people in Africa have died from Aids.

## 8 Can the Aids virus be tested for straightaway?

You need to have a blood test in order to tell whether or not you have been infected by the Aids virus, but it can take at least 4 months after the infection for the test to become positive.

## 9 Does infection with the Aids virus last for ever?

Yes, probably. Once you've got the Aids virus, it appears that you have it for the rest of your life.

## 10 If you're infected with the Aids virus, do you get ill immediately?

No. You may be infected with the virus and show no signs of illness for years – maybe in some cases, never. However, even if you are not ill, YOU WILL STILL BE INFECTIOUS TO OTHERS.

## 11 Do all people infected with the Aids virus die from it?

At the moment some people who are infected with the virus do not seem to develop the disease. However, year by year, of all the people who have the virus infection, gradually more and more do develop the disease. Once someone has developed the disease, the chances of dying are high because at the moment there is no cure – although there are now better drugs available that help deal with the symptoms.

## 12 What are the symptoms?

The first signs of being ill with the Aids disease can be very vague and very much like other illnesses. Tiredness and swollen glands are common, but having these doesn't mean you've got Aids. Other symptoms are loss of weight and repeated infections. Whether or not you are worried about having Aids will depend upon what you have been doing and whether you have put yourself at risk of getting it.

### 13 Is there a cure?

No, and no immediate likelihood of there being one. There are drugs that slow the disease down, though. Scientists are also working on developing a vaccine to protect against Aids.

### 14 Can the Aids virus be passed on even if you don't know you have it?

Yes. The blood test only becomes positive several months after the virus has gone into the body. Not everyone infected with the virus knows that they've got it, because they won't have had a blood test.

### 15 Where will the virus be in someone who is infected?

In their blood, semen, vaginal secretions. It can also be found in saliva, faeces, tears and urine – but only in very small amounts and it is not thought that you can catch it from them.

### 16 How can a person catch the Aids virus?

From an infected person by: sharing needles, anal intercourse, an infected mother to her unborn baby, vaginal intercourse. Some people in the past have caught Aids by being given a blood transfusion with infected blood or infected blood products, but all blood and blood products in the UK are now tested.

You CANNOT catch it by: touching doorknobs, sharing dishes and glasses, using lavatory seats, holding hands, having head lice, sneezing and coughing, and swimming in swimming pools. So far, it is thought that you CANNOT catch it by: kissing or sharing toothbrushes.

## 17 When having sex…

A man can catch the Aids virus from an infected man or woman.

A woman can catch it from an infected man.

There are no known cases of a woman catching it from an infected woman.

## 18 Groups of people most at risk:

The groups of people most at risk in Britain were homosexuals and bisexuals, intravenous (injecting) drug users and prostitutes; and, previously, people having blood transfusions and haemophiliacs. But now, increasingly, it is also someone having sex with someone of the opposite sex without using a condom. It's certainly not just a gay disease – the most recent survey shows 45% of people now being diagnosed with Aids in the UK are from sex between a man and a woman. Sex between two men and intravenous drug using are responsible for most of the other cases.

## 19 What kills the Aids virus?

The Aids virus is very sensitive, and outside the body it doesn't survive very well. It is also killed off by heat, soap and water, and disinfectants. This is why you cannot catch Aids from an infected person from cups, doorknobs and lavatory seats.

## 20 Do condoms protect you from catching Aids?

Yes – almost completely. It is a very good idea to use them always. REMEMBER THEY ALSO PROTECT YOU FROM OTHER SEXUALLY TRANSMITTED DISEASES AND FROM PREGNANCY.

## 21 Who can you go to for help?

If you have reason to be really worried that you might have Aids, the only way to find out if you are or are not infected with the virus is to have a blood test, and for that you need to see a doctor.

---

## 22 What worries you most?

The survey of your class showed that the top four worries were:

(1) a terrorist attack

(2) a parent or brother or sister dying

(3) failing your exams

(4) not having a 'steady' friend of the opposite sex.

Not surprisingly, this is very different for different people at different times. There is no right or wrong thing to worry about.

---

When Pete's class were asked this a few years ago the number 1 worry was being unemployed. Mark (rated by me as only 2/10) seemed to know all the answers. Not surprising, seeing his reputation with the girls. I'd have to be really desperate to say 'yes' to him!

We had this discussion about Aids at supper on Friday evening and Sal was there. I asked Sal about her boyfriends in the past year, and Sal counted on the fingers of both hands – just to wind Mum up. Mum went spare, so to calm her down I asked how many boyfriends she'd had before she met Dad. Mum started to count on the fingers of both her hands too, and when she saw the look on Dad's face she burst out laughing.

Just thinking about Mum and Dad having sex turns me off, though it must have happened for Pete and me to be here. But surely they can't still be at it??

**9th November** What a weekend. Got up at 5 a.m. on Saturday morning and took a taxi to Waterloo station. Dad's behaving as if he's really rich. Then caught the Eurostar train to Paris, with me being a real 'know-all' because I'd been there already. Stayed in a tiny, brilliant hotel called 'Monsieur Le Prince' (though didn't see any princes around – but could've done with Prince William, who I think is – no can't even think about it given he's a Royal). It was in some place called St Germain, which I hadn't been to when I was there before. Pete is going to be dead jealous. Mum and Dad had a big argument about whether to spend all the time doing le shopping or going to things like the Eiffel Tower. Ended up by doing both. I bought some brilliant scent called Caleche, which I reckon makes me smell dead nice…not that I have anyone sniffing at me just at the moment. Went to all sorts of places like the Rodin museum, which was stuffed with statues of people kissing one another. And then to some museum called the Key D'Orsay or something – I am so stuffed with culture I never want to see another picture again. What I liked best was sitting around with Mum and Dad in cafés sipping café au lait and looking at les boys going by. Came back Sunday night but slept all the way. Reckon Dad's brilliant. But, but – that's not all…

CHARLIE'S PHONED! He really meant it about not phoning me because he didn't have my number. Wish he'd phoned before and I would've asked Dad whether he could come to Paris with us. Anyhow I'm seeing him next week. Why does it have to be so long away? Txt-messaged him 'C\ W8 2 C U – Susie'. And just as the little square disappeared up into the right-hand corner of my mobile screen saying it had been sent – I wished it hadn't.

# In Need of
## Financial Aids

**21st November** Still missing Pete – much to my surprise. Even the teasing. He rang because he's short of money as usual. Told him all about Paris to make him dead envious. He reckons that Dad should give him the money that he'd saved by not taking him.

My money situation is crucial too. Spent a fortune (which I didn't have) in Paris. Don't think I get enough pocket-money, so did a quick survey among my friends. Kate only gets £2.50 a week – don't know how she manages, but of course she doesn't buy her own clothes or anything. Mary gets the most. Her parents are divorced too, and she gets £15 a week from her mum AND £15 from her dad. She says she bids them up against one another and makes the other one feel guilty. Most of us seem to get around £10 a week, which is what I'm meant to get – when Mum remembers. Did get this as an allowance of £40 a month, but then I'd blow it all the first day. Mum says it's only for the cinema, presents, CDs, bus fares, make-up and magazines. She buys the clothes and shoes.

Seeing that we work at school, I reckon we ought to get paid for going there. Then I'd be independent of having to ask Mum for the money all the time. Charlie's working as a garage mechanic apprentice and making £140 a week. Sounded like a fortune till he pointed out how much goes on tax, and then he pays his mum and dad £40 a week for food and lodging. Also he has to pay for his travel, his own clothes, AND for taking me to the cinema! I said I'd pay for myself the first time, and then found I couldn't as I didn't have any money! Reckon it's the thought that counts though.

I used to be richer when I did babysitting, but I've been put off doing that now. I could get a job like Mary. She works as a glass-collector in a wine bar on Saturday and Sunday nights. She's under 18, so they don't have to pay the minimum wage and she only gets £6.00 for two and a half hours. I can't wait till I'm 18, because they'll have to pay me at least £3.50 an hour, and when I'm over 21 it'll be £4.10 an hour.

**22nd November** A letter from Pete! Maybe he misses ME!

*Dear Susie,*

*Well, here I am, a real university student at last – even if I'm broke. Reckon I'm going to need to take out a huge student loan like everyone else here. After you and Mum left, panic set in. Would anyone like me? What if no one talks to me? Would they all be cleverer than me? Began to think 'I'm going to drop out. I want a year off'.*

*Anyhow Mum was great when I rang up. You know how understanding she can be when she wants. 'You'll be fine, everyone is in the same boat. Just be yourself.' The soundest piece of advice, that. There was mail waiting for me (god I'm so popular, I thought, as I filled a carrier bag with it all). The letters were all about me joining some society or other – not one personal one amongst the lot.*

*My room. Mmmmmh, not bad – small and a bit smelly. Thought a few posters would do the trick. I didn't unpack, but went out to find some people to meet. I wasn't going to* spend the next 5 years all on my ownsome, was I? Didn't know a soul. Kept telling myself 'Impose yourself' – 'Hi, I'm Pete, how's it going?' 'Have a nice day.' Suddenly it didn't seem so easy, but I've made some friends and I'll tell you about them when I see you at Christmas.

Missing you all, and my room back home, and you'd better all write to me. Could you get Mum to send me all the latest football clippings from the back of the local rag? Could you send me my blue pullover from the top drawer in my room (it might need a bit of a wash first), also my other pair of shoes, my folder with the lined paper, and my second pen – the one with the chewed end. Plus my medical dictionary, and the book on medical geniuses. If all this is too much trouble, you could give them all to Sandy, who's coming up to see me next week – I hope.

Love from your brother
Health Freak Pete

PS Am sharing a kitchen with a bloke who's managed to create an ideology to defend the fact that he's a lazy bastard. He never cleans up after himself. I'm going to use this excuse when I get back home.

PPS Forgot to post this letter when I wrote it 5 weeks ago! Sorry to hear Bov ate Pinko. Was hoping to experiment on Pinko when I came back at Christmas. You really should have been more careful – it's cruel to rabbits to allow cats to eat them, you know.

Pete doesn't know about Charlie yet. Not sure I do really. I had a great time at the cinema last night. No attempted rape!

**26th November** Aids, Aids, Aids. Can't see why they call it Aids when it doesn't aid anyone. Mary reckons that Mini Willie's attitude to Aids is: 'I'll have to cut down on the girlies, and if I do have to jump into bed for a bonk then I'll use a johnny, cos I can't do without it altogether.'

I don't know one person with Aids – but had to spend whole afternoon at school talking about it, chlamydia (another sex nasty) and relationships today. Quite revealing about some of my friends. John said 'If I caught it, I would try to make the rest of my life more exciting and just as I wanted it. I wouldn't sleep with anybody else so that no one else would catch it from me. I don't think I'd tell anyone – just go to a place where other people had Aids, so I wouldn't feel so cast out.'

Mary was really awful and said if she caught Aids, she'd try to give it to as many people as possible and try to take them with her.

While we were talking, a scribbled note was passed from Kate, who sits in front of me, saying:

> 'Aids advice – don't be silly
> Put a condom on his willy.'

As I was laughing, Mr Rogers (remember the bad breath?) found me with it. He read it, went bright red, and then collapsed trying not to laugh too. He had been explaining that the chances of a man without the Aids virus catching it from a woman with the virus, during one-off sexual intercourse, was about 1 in 1,000, and the other way round (we women always have it worse) was 1 in 100. But most people don't just have sex only once!

Emma thought that Aids had changed her outlook on sex, and though it wouldn't scare her away from having sex altogether, she reckoned that it might make her more cautious when she started. She'd be sure to know the person she was having sex with, and would want to ask her partner about his previous sex life. She was worried, though, that he might think it a bit rude and offensive. Mr Rogers said we shouldn't be afraid to ask what other sexual partners someone had had. It might make all the difference between life and death. And it wasn't just because of Aids, but because of all the other sexually transmitted diseases you could get as well – like chlamydia, which is what really scares me, as you seem to be able to catch it and not know till you try to get pregnant and find your tubes are all blocked up.

OK, so I wish the scientists would find a cure for Aids. It's incredibly frightening to think that if you go with someone, you don't know whether they have got it or not. Must have been much, much more people killed from Aids than from terrorism, I reckon.

What I hate most is seeing babies on television who have been born with Aids. They don't even know that they have it, but they are going to die, which is really depressing, because the amount of people who are catching Aids is still going up. What I particularly didn't like was the programme about a man who was so angry that he was going to die from Aids that he went with everybody he could, so as to spread the disease. I think that's really selfish – like what Mary said. I also watched this play about a man who caught Aids. He had to tell his wife how he'd caught it, by going with another man. He got worse and worse. I think this programme must have got across to a lot of people, if they didn't forget it after a couple of weeks.

'Thought for the Day' written on our toilet wall at school: 'Last one to get Aids is a wanker'.

**29th November** I think it's going well with Charlie — at least I hope so. I hardly dare write about it or tell anybody about him, in case it all goes pear-shaped. Sometimes I worry about whether he does fancy me — he's so unpushy. Today I found a four-leaf clover, so everything is bound to be OK.

**3rd December** Don't know how Pete manages it — wanting to be a doctor. I think I'd be hopeless. I needed Pete's expertise this morning but it was Sita who knew what to do.

We were all outside, between lessons, me avoiding the usual crowd in one corner smoking fags, when suddenly this boy from year 9 fell to the ground and started jerking around. I think everyone thought he was joking to begin with, but then a crowd gathered round and just stared. No one knew what to do and we were all getting scared, thinking he was dying or something, when Sita pushed past me and told everyone to stand back and not to touch him and that he'd be all right. I was dead impressed.

The boy stopped jerking after what seemed ages, but was probably only a minute. Then he seemed to go to sleep. Sita pushed him onto his side, and said this was so that he wouldn't breathe in his sick if he threw up. She said you should do that if someone was unconscious for any reason.

Mr Rogers arrived at this point and sent everyone back into their classrooms — Sita too, which seemed a bit unfair as she had done everything properly. Afterwards Sita said she had a cousin who used to have fits when he was little, but it only happened when he got a high temperature. Mr Rogers came and said 'thank you' to her later, and explained that the boy had had epilepsy for some time. Normally he didn't have any problems, as long as he took his tablets every morning, but he had obviously forgotten for the last few days.

I think Mr Rogers knew we were all scared because he reassured us that epilepsy affects about 5 people in every 1,000. With medicines, most people with epilepsy can live perfectly normal lives today, as long as people let them. The worst problem that epileptics have to put up with is other people being frightened of them and treating them as if they are ill all the time or mental or something. They can do everything everybody else does. They can do jobs, play sports, even swim (as long as they are with somebody).

But it was scary, and I can see how people think epileptics might die when they are having an attack. Mr Rogers said that that was very rare. He said if you see someone having an attack, you have to make sure they can't hurt themselves against anything while they are jerking about. He said that people used to think they should put something into epileptic's mouths to stop them biting their tongue. This is now thought to be wrong, because they might choke on it, or they might bite you by mistake. If you leave them alone, the attack will stop after a few minutes. Then you should do what Sita had done, and lay them on their side, till they wake up. Normally they don't have to go to hospital or anything, and Sita and I even saw the boy back in the playground in the afternoon.

I think maybe he should have said 'thank you' or something to Sita, but maybe he didn't know it was her who had helped him, or maybe he was embarrassed. Pete's home next week, so I'll be able to tell him about it.

# An Itchy
## and Freaky **Christmas**

**10th December** Pete's home. His usual arrogant little self, and worse 'know-all' now he's at university. Didn't tell him I saw Sandy snogging James last week. I do mind for him but don't want to be the person to have to tell him.

I did tell him about the boy having an epileptic fit in school. Nice to be able to tell HIM something for a change.

**17th December** Pete's birthday. He's 19! He's not having a party at home as he had one in Nottingham last week.

**18th December** Charlie's been away on a training course for two weeks. Now he's back, we're seeing quite a lot of one another. Mum won't let me see him during the week in term time as she thinks it interferes with my work, so my mobile has been humming with txt messages. Although I get angry with Mum, and argue with her about this, actually it's quite good. I can get on with my work and tell Charlie it's all Mum's fault!

All that stuff Pete said about 'sexual sequencing' seems to be true, though I hadn't really considered it before. I thought it was something that only happened to other people, or in books. It certainly never occurs to me in the heat of the action!

I know that Charlie fancies me because he's always looking at me out of the corner of his eye. His hand sometimes brushes against mine as if by accident. He smiles at me a lot, and sits close to me when there are other seats around. He certainly looks at other parts of my body! Wonder if boys always look at girls' breasts or whether it is just me. Also he's always nervously checking to see how I respond to what he is saying. Sometimes he even agrees with what I say when I know he really doesn't think the same way. I thought only girls did this! He always seems to be licking his lips, which makes me wonder what he's expecting, and though he's kissed me, I don't think he's got much experience – but then neither had I until recently!

I was wrong about him being into drugs – he's like Pete about that kind of thing, though he did say he'd smoked cannabis a couple of times. He said that it was just to see what it was like and it didn't do anything for him anyway.

**20th December** Pete's a problem at the moment. Things are not good between him and Sandy. He thinks she's two-timing him, which she is. He can't understand what girls are about. He has a long list of complaints like: 'Why can't she say what she wants?' 'Why does she have to keep crying and hinting there's some terrible dark secret?' 'Why does she keep saying she'll tell me about it and then doesn't?' He thinks she's trying to tantalize him. Then after being really mean to him, she is suddenly all over him again. She became really angry when Pete rejected her last time she tried this. Pete doesn't deserve to be treated like that. He's worth more than the Sandys of this world and I told him he should drop her.

Showed Pete the Aids questionnaire. He got half the questions wrong, but said it didn't matter as he wasn't in the high-risk group. I sometimes wonder. Anyway, I told him it *did* matter, as not only people in the high-risk group get Aids. So I gave him the answer sheet as well.

Pete has learnt something at medical school about sexually transmitted diseases, though he's not sure how useful some of it would be today. Apparently they used to treat syphilis by applying a roast turnip 'as hot as the patient can bear' to the 'affected part'. I asked him all innocent like, 'What part's that?'

He and I used his calculator to work out that if you slept with five different people in a year, and they each slept with five people, and so on, then you could be spreading Aids to 3,905 people other people over 5 years. Twenty partners and it worked out at around three million.

**23rd December** Pete's always worrying about his health. I think it's all to do with Sandy's dad having died from a heart attack. He was only 56 but smoked 20 a day and 'liked' his food. Pete wants to have the amount of cholesterol in his blood measured. He's sure it must be high. He's heard that most heart attacks are caused by having too much cholesterol in your blood. Apparently loads of people (70%) have a high cholesterol level in this country, which is why they think so many people die of heart attacks.

Asked him what I should do to avoid having a heart attack when I was old like Mum. Shouldn't have asked, should I? Not if I didn't want a half-hour lecture from Pete. He said I had to start eating wholemeal bread, wholemeal pasta, beans, baked potatoes in their jackets, lentils, brown rice, 5 pieces of fruit and veg a day (which I already do)...

I begged to go to the lav, it was the talk of all that fibre that did it, I swear, but the avalanche had begun and wasn't to be diverted. My lav avalanche would just have to wait.

'...take more regular exercise, drink skimmed milk rather than the full-fat stuff, use low-fat yoghurt instead of cream, use sunflower spreads instead of butter, cook in polyunsaturated vegetable oil and drain it off the food afterwards, eat more fish, the white bits of the chicken (not the skin), and less red meat...'

Please, please, please I'm bursting!

'...grilled rather than fried food, no chips or sausages, no salt added at the table. We can make do with one-tenth of the salt we eat at the moment.'

How did he know all these things? He's like a flipping encyclopedia.

'It's really up to us. While we want chips, they'll sell chips. If our Health Service is meant to be doing all this preventative stuff and making us eat better, then why isn't the government helping by at least making sure that all school meals are healthy?'

Just made it to the lav in time. When I got back, I told him about my success at school with the food questionnaire. Think he was nearly impressed, but, as always, came back with more facts. How does he remember them all? Apparently teenage boys need about 2,500 calories per day, and teenage girls about 2,000 (and less than 30% of these calories should come from fat). And if they take lots of exercise, they need more.

Poor Pete, he's got a letter from Sandy and it's all off. Must be why Bov chose today to eat the two goldfish – first Pinko and now Leroy and Marvin. Leroy and Marvin had been given him by Sandy – so Bov must've got some vibes that things were off between Sandy and him. Told Pete that it was better for the fish than just Petering out, ha ha. He was not amused, and in fact I thought he was going to cry. Thought that boys didn't do that sort of thing.

**24th December** Daisy, Paul and Aunty Jo came for a Christmas tea. They're staying with Aunty Pam so we'll see them again tomorrow. Aunty Jo's getting a divorce. Uncle Geoff's back from a spell with some United Nations force and off with his floozie. Pity he didn't get blown up – the way he's treated Aunty Jo. Mum was horrified when I said that.

**25th December** What a Christmas present. Woke up with an itchy bum. Must be worms again. Surely I'm too old for worms. Bet it's from my cousins. I catch everything from them.

Dad says you can't get worms that quickly. Real expert on all the nasty things we get, but doesn't seem to be able to stop us catching them though. Says human worms come in almost as many varieties as Ben and Jerry's ice-cream – put me right off eating the stuff. There are long worms, short ones, thin ones, fat ones and flat ones. There are worms that travel round your body and lay eggs everywhere, ones that make you thin, ones that make your bum itch, ones that are caught from animals, ones that are caught from eating uncooked food, ones that are caught from other human beings – on and on. The commonest one is the thread worm (also known as the pin worm or *Enterobius vermicularis* – but most commonly referred to as just 'the worms'), which Dad said was the one I had.

He talks about them as if they were almost friendly! 'The thread worm is an innocuous little thing that inhabits the insides of about one in three of us at any time. They come in two sexes, and the "hers" are bigger than the "hims" – 13 millimetres compared with 5 mm, and with a diameter of 0.5 mm compared with 0.2 mm. The poor old pregnant worm is really just made up of two huge wombs – ready to spill out – while all the male has for himself is a curly tail! They mainly live in your gut, near your appendix, and the female creeps out at night to lay her eggs on the skin around your bottom, which is why yours is itching.' Thanks for all that, Dad – real Christmas present.

Dad said I'd got worms from someone who had scratched their own bum because it was itchy. They'd got the eggs under their fingernails, and then touched some food which I'd eaten, so it had all got spread around. Yugh. Don't like the idea that I've eaten something from someone else's bum. Now they're squirming around inside me having a Christmas feast.

All I have to do is take some anti-worm medicine, but I can't go to the chemist because they're all closed. The whole family will have to take the medicine – like the anti-louse stuff.

Pete says he's got them too. He wanted to use this as an excuse for us not to go to Aunty Pam's for lunch. No way Mum was going to let us off. She said it was up to us, BUT…

Aunty Pam and Uncle Bob's house was reeking of the usual resident dog shit and cat pee. I sometimes wonder whether it's always the same turd and piddle that they've never cleaned up from one year to the next.

There was a 4-hour interval before the meal was served up. All jolly Christmas spirit had sunk to zero. What with Uncle Bob being plastered, Gran snoring, Dad with nothing left to say, Mum trying to fill in the 10-minute conversational gaps, Aunty Jo sobbing quietly, Aunty Pam in the kitchen swearing, Daisy reading Aunty Pam's old knitting patterns…Pete and Paul completely disappeared and I just sat and scratched my bum.

I think Sal was right to go to her boyfriend's parents for Christmas. Wish I could have gone with her.

When the meal finally came, no one could find Pete and Paul. I said they were probably upstairs smoking a spliff of that 'Chaos' stuff and getting high together. Mum looked at me with a definite question mark on her face but didn't say anything. Daisy rushed upstairs (I think she wanted to try some too) but only found Dad, smoking a fag.

We finally found the boys in the garden playing football. They came in covered with mud and trod more dog shit into the new carpet. Paul tripped over the electric wire to the Christmas tree lights, and the tree fell onto the table. The result was 'needle soup'. Don't think it made it any worse. Aunty Pam definitely wins the Decrepit Aunts' 'Worst Cook of the Year' prize. I'm glad I'm a vegetarian. Uncle Bob's carving was more gruesome than the latest horror movie and Aunty Pam had left the plastic bag of innards inside the turkey.

We had the wettest crackers I've ever known. Not one banger worked. Only Aunty Pam and Uncle Bob would wear their paper hats. Everyone else complained that they were too small. I wonder whether they find special morons to write the cracker jokes?

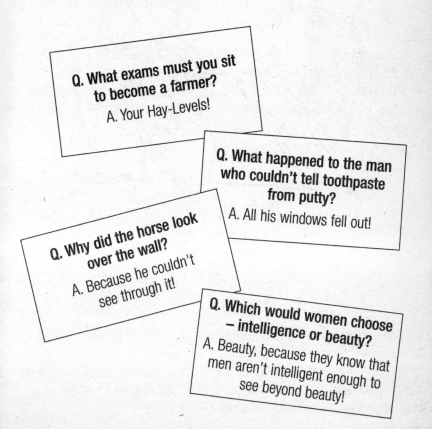

Q. What exams must you sit to become a farmer?
A. Your Hay-Levels!

Q. What happened to the man who couldn't tell toothpaste from putty?
A. All his windows fell out!

Q. Why did the horse look over the wall?
A. Because he couldn't see through it!

Q. Which would women choose – intelligence or beauty?
A. Beauty, because they know that men aren't intelligent enough to see beyond beauty!

Pete frisked the plum pudding for money, but Aunty Pam's far too mean to put in anything more than 5p's, one of which Daisy swallowed, so it's just as well we're not into Euros yet. There was no brandy left to light it with, because Uncle Bob had drunk it all. He was so pissed, he even forgot to ask if I'd got a boyfriend yet. The only time I had wanted him to ask, too. Just so I could say 'Yes' at last!

# Index